WONDERS OF MAN

THE KREMLIN

by Abraham Ascher

and the Editors
of the Newsweek Book Division

NEWSWEEK, New York

NEWSWEEK BOOK DIVISION

JOSEPH L. GARDNER   *Editor*

Janet Czarnetzki   *Art Director*
Edwin D. Bayrd, Jr.   *Associate Editor*
Laurie P. Phillips   *Picture Editor*
Eva Galan   *Assistant Editor*
Lynne H. Brown   *Copy Editor*
Russell Ash   *European Correspondent*

S. ARTHUR DEMBNER   *Publisher*

WONDERS OF MAN

MILTON GENDEL   *Consulting Editor*

Library of Congress Catalog Card No. 79-163361
© 1972—Arnoldo Mondadori Editore, S.p.A.
All rights reserved. Printed and bound in Italy.

Title page:
The branches of the "Tree of the State of Moscow" encircle a representation of the Vladimir Madonna, Russia's holiest icon. Portraits of Moscow's earliest rulers festoon the limbs that overarch the pink walls of the Kremlin.
Opposite:
An elaborately illuminated menu from the coronation feast of Nicholas II, last tsar of Russia, and his wife, Alexandra.

Contents

Introduction

The massive walls, gilded onion domes, and truncated towers of the Moscow Kremlin have dominated that city's skyline for more than eight hundred years. The original fortress, built by Prince Iuri Dolgoruki in 1156, was little more than a crude wooden stockade set on a high, forested bluff overlooking the confluence of the Moscow and Neglinnaia rivers. Over the centuries that first insubstantial *kremlin*, or citadel, was repeatedly gutted by fire and sacked by Tatar warriors.

Rebuilt and expanded a half dozen times, the Kremlin's twenty-foot-thick battlements have stood as mute witness to the epochal events in Russian history: the consolidation of the Muscovite empire, the protracted struggle against the Golden Horde, and the nefarious excesses of Ivan the Terrible's reign.

As the clustered cupolas of Russia's holiest churches indicate, the Kremlin was the seat of ecclesiastical as well as temporal power in ancient times. And even after the capital was formally transferred to St. Petersburg in 1718, Russian monarchs continued to use the Kremlin on state occasions. Peter the Great chose Moscow — rather than his "window to the West" — for the coronation of his second wife, and Catherine the Great elected to execute the rebel Pugachev at the Kremlin. Forty-seven tsars are buried within its walls; an even greater number were crowned there, among them Nicholas II, last Tsar of All the Russias.

During the opening days of the Revolution of 1917, Bolshevik forces shelled the Kremlin, damaging several of its towers. Fully restored before the fifty-first anniversary of the Revolution (left), the sixty-six-acre compound serves today as the epicenter of the Soviet state.

THE EDITORS

11

Ivan IV's victorious armies return to Moscow (left) after their victory over the Mongols at Kazan (right).

THE KREMLIN
IN HISTORY

I

A Citadel of Wood

"What man ever thought or divined that Moscow would become a kingdom, or what man ever thought that Moscow would be considered an Empire?" This question, the opening line of an epic tale that was extremely popular in the seventeenth century, epitomizes the Russian people's astonishment over the growth of the Muscovite kremlin — which was initially identical to the town of Moscow — into the capital of their powerful state. Today that contrast is even more pronounced, for over the centuries the Kremlin has evolved into the nerve center of world communism. As such, the conglomeration of buildings that dominates the metropolis of 6,000,000 has inspired hope, awe, or terror in the hearts of millions of people. Many view its occupants as the saviors of mankind from all worldly injustice; others look upon them as instigators of revolutions and practitioners of violence. Despite these developments our knowledge of the origins of the Kremlin is sketchy, not much more extensive than it was in the seventeenth century. Like so much else about Russia, the earliest history of the Kremlin seems to be "a riddle wrapped in a mystery inside an enigma."

The question of the Kremlin's origins is especially intriguing because in the course of two centuries it enjoyed a spectacular rise from obscurity to prominence. Eight hundred years ago, during the heyday of the loose confederation of principalities known as Kievan Russia, many cities were built around a *kremlin,* or fortress, but at that time few Russians had heard of the one in remote Moscow. The citadels of Kiev, Novgorod, Tver, and Vladimir overshadowed it by far, and although archaeological evidence suggests the existence of a settled community in Moscow in antiquity, the town is not mentioned in the Russian Chronicles until 1147, and then only briefly. Yet beginning in the late fourteenth century, the rulers who lived in the Muscovite kremlin often determined the fate of the whole country.

Aside from its political importance, the Kremlin engages our interest because of its architectural splendor. Shaped like an irregular pentagon and bounded on two sides by the Moscow and Neglinnaia rivers, it encompasses a 65-acre hill that rises to a height of 125 feet at its center. Massive walls, ranging in thickness from 12 to 16 feet, surround the citadel; no fewer than 19 exquisitely ornamented towers — the tallest and most elegant of which is the 238-foot Savior's Tower — jut out from these walls. Most impressive of all is the bewildering array of structures from different historical eras that stand within the confines of the Kremlin: magnificent cathedrals, monasteries, luxurious palaces, a theater, a historical museum, a modern office building, and the Palace of Soviets. Many of Russia's most valuable artistic and historical treasures are housed there.

Lacking reliable information about the origins of their capital, the Russian people compensated by inventing fanciful legends and folktales to explain its rise. One of the better known tales gives the fullest account. According to that legend, Prince Daniel of Suzdal is said to have chanced upon the "beautiful hamlets of the goodly *boyar* [high-ranking nobleman] Stephen Ivanovich Kuchka" near the Moscow River in 1180. Kuchka's two sons ("in all the Russian lands there were no such beautiful youngsters") pleased the prince, and he invited them to serve at his court. Reluctantly, Stephen agreed to his sons' departure — a decision he was soon to regret. Although the young men enjoyed

Daniel's favor and were quickly promoted to important posts, they succumbed to the evil temptations of the prince's wife, Ulita, a passionate woman purportedly inspired by the Devil. Fearing that their shameful adultery might be discovered by the prince, the three sinners decided to murder him. The Kuchka brothers secretly stalked their prey while he was on a solitary hunting trip, savagely speared him to death, cut off his head, and concealed his body in a secluded hut. To prove that the deed had been done, they presented the prince's bloodstained clothes to Ulita — and then resumed their life of adultery.

So dastardly a crime could not go unpunished, and thus when Prince Andrew of Vladimir, Daniel's brother, heard of it he gathered together an army and marched on Suzdal, where he apprehended Ulita and executed her "by all manner of torture." He then pursued the Kuchkas to their father's estate, and in short order he cruelly tortured both the father and his sons to death. Having meted out justice, Andrew surveyed Kuchka's lands and found them appealing. At that point "God put it into his heart" to build a city on the site — a suggestion the good prince was too pious to ignore. Thus Moscow was founded. According to the legend, it was even then believed to be destined for a great future.

Although this legend is largely apocryphal, it does contain certain elements of truth. Apparently a family of boyars named Kuchka did live in the Moscow region at one time. They gave their name to a small rural district that was still referred to in the fifteenth century as Kuchkovo pole (Kuchka's Field), and as late as the seventeenth century the Moscow River was widely known as "Moscow, the Kuchka river." But the history of the Kuchkas, like that of Moscow itself, is shrouded in mystery and the improbabilities of ancient legend.

When compared with this stirring legend, the few substantiated facts about the origins of the Moscow Kremlin seem rather colorless. The Russian Chronicles relate that in 1147 Iuri Dolgoruki (George of the Long Arm), Prince of Suzdal, invited his ally, Prince Sviatoslav of Novgorod–Seversk, to Moscow. The host entertained his guest with a "mighty dinner"; thus we may presume the existence of a structure of some consequence there. Nine years later Iuri laid the foundation of Moscow by constructing a wooden wall around that building. This small fortress, situated at the western corner of Kremlin Hill, comprised one third or at most one half of the territory that the citadel occupies today.

For about a century the town was assigned to junior princes, none of whom stayed very long or did much to promote its growth. During the last decades of that century Prince Gleb of Riazan came upon Moscow and burned the entire town and its surrounding villages, and as the era drew to a close Moscow was sacked by the Tatars (or Mongols), a fate that befell much of Kievan Russia in the 1230's and 1240's. The Tatar domination of Russia, which was to last for almost 250 years, belongs to one of the most remarkable sagas of conquest in the annals of mankind. Over that period, 1,000,000 Tatars led by a highly disciplined and magnificently trained army of roughly 200,000 warriors, were to extend their rule over 100,000,000 people. Their empire stretched from the shores of the Pacific Ocean to the Adriatic coast, from China to Hungary.

The Tatars, whose original habitat was present-day

Mongolia, did not interfere directly in Russian life, but they did demand regular payments of tribute and recruits for their army. One of the few cities in Russia to escape devastation during their domination was Novgorod, which owed its good fortune to the courage and acuity of its ruler, Alexander Nevsky. Threatened at the time by the Swedes and Teutonic knights, as well as by the Tatars, Alexander shrewdly decided to fight only those he thought he could defeat.

To this end Alexander directed his first blow against the Swedes. In 1240 the two armies met on the banks of the Neva River (from which Alexander took the honorific eponym Nevsky), and there the Russians inflicted a crushing defeat on the invaders. Fighting in the front lines, Alexander himself wounded the Swedish commander and almost fell into enemy hands. Two years later he routed the Teutonic knights on the ice of Lake Peipus, an epic victory that has been repeatedly celebrated in songs and stories, in Prokofiev's music, and in a superb film by Russian director Sergei Eisenstein. At first, the Germans seemed to be overpowering the Novgorodian army, but at the decisive moment Alexander led a savage attack against the enemy flank that completely reversed the situation. At the same moment the spring ice suddenly broke, and many Germans were delivered into the frigid waters of the lake.

Despite the success of this "massacre on the ice," Alexander entertained no illusions about his military strength. When a Tatar raiding party encamped on the outskirts of Novgorod, Alexander persuaded the Novgorodians to pay the tribute they demanded — a realistic policy that spared the city from destruction and set an example for later Muscovite rulers. (Three cen-turies after his death the Orthodox Church canonized Alexander for having kept both the Roman Catholics and the Tatars at bay.)

It was only during the second half of the thirteenth century, when Alexander's youngest son, Daniel, became ruler of Moscow, that the city was considered the capital of a permanent principality. Daniel inherited his father's ability, but he was ambitious and ruthless as well. His favorite stratagem seems to have been to extend his meager holdings at the expense of neighboring princes. On one occasion, for example, he invited a rival to dinner and promptly threw him into jail, after which he appropriated his hapless and unsuspecting guest's land. By the time Daniel died in 1303, he controlled the mouth of the Moscow River, a strategically and commercially important region. In area, however, his holdings did not comprise more than five hundred square miles.

Daniel's descendants remained in Moscow, whose favorable geography now made it a haven for colonists and a center of trade. The town's proximity to the headwaters of four major rivers — the Oka, Volga, Don, and Dnieper — facilitated commerce with various parts of Russia. Close also to several major overland routes, Moscow evolved into a natural depot for refugees fleeing the declining Kievan region, which had been repeatedly attacked by Tatar hordes. Moreover, the city's location deep within the Kievan federation endowed it with a measure of military security. The enemy would attack surrounding cities and then, either exhausted or content with their plunder, would fall back without proceeding to Moscow. Between 1238 and 1368 the city was sacked only once, in 1293; no other city in northern

Russia escaped enemy attack for as long a time.

The princes of Moscow made the most of these natural advantages. As junior princes they could not even aspire to the throne of a major principality and therefore devoted all their energies to expanding their patrimony, generally by the most expedient means. One of Russia's most accomplished historians has aptly referred to the earliest rulers of Moscow as "robbers of the most unblushing type." But in addition they were crafty opportunists. If they observed that a neighboring prince was momentarily weak, they attacked him without provocation. On other occasions they resorted to treaties or outright purchase in order to enlarge their territory. Although most of them were neither colorful nor exceptionally gifted, the Muscovite princes seemed to instinctively accommodate their policies to the often changing circumstances. They rarely undertook an action for which they were too weak, and they did not shrink from forming alliances with the heathen "devourers of raw flesh," their Tatar oppressors. In short, steadiness, caution, flexibility, and moderation were the hallmarks of their policies. As one commentator noted somewhat ruefully, they did not even carry their "tendency to get drunk after dinner" to excess.

No one exemplified these traits more strikingly than Ivan I, nicknamed Kalita or "Moneybags," who ruled Moscow from 1328 to 1340. Some historians believe that he received this name because of his stinginess, but in many folktales Ivan is depicted as a generous prince who always carried a moneybag so that on his travels he could distribute alms to the poor. Whatever the real reason for his name, he was certainly shrewd in handling money. His lavish gifts to the Khan of the

Golden Horde (ruler of the autonomous Tatar state on the lower Volga) were designed to ensure his principality against attack.

Ivan had ingratiated himself with the Golden Horde in 1327 when he led an army against his own countrymen in retaliation for their refusal to pay the tribute demanded of them. As a reward for his victory over the principality of Tver, the khan bestowed on Kalita the title Grand Prince of Vladimir, a position of great prestige that for a hundred years was retained uninterruptedly by the Muscovite rulers. Kalita then assumed responsibility for collecting tribute throughout northern Russia. He performed this task efficiently and ruthlessly, always making sure that some of the funds remained in his own coffers. These profits went toward purchasing additional land, which Ivan acquired from impecunious princes, private landlords, and ecclesiastical institutions. The khan, grateful to be relieved of the burden of collecting the tribute himself, gave his blessing to Ivan's unremitting accumulation of territory.

In the long run, one of the most significant aspects of Ivan's reign was the transformation of Moscow into the spiritual center of the nation. (Even before the founding of Moscow the Russians had been converted — about 988 — to the Orthodox Christianity whose principal center was Constantinople.) The repeated Tatar incursions into Kiev had induced Metropolitan Maxim to abandon that city in favor of Vladimir in 1299. The choice had proven unfortunate, however, for the secular authorities and the metropolitan had begun to quarrel, a situation that was soon exploited by Ivan's brother Iuri, then ruler of Moscow, who established cordial relations with Maxim's successor, Peter.

During his visit to Moscow in 1326 Peter had died, an event that later metropolitans interpreted as evidence of divine selection of the city to be the seat of the Russian Church. One legend that gained currency in the late fourteenth century maintained that Peter actually died in Ivan's arms after uttering the following prophesy:

> My son, if thou shouldst hearken unto me, and shouldst build the Church of the Holy Mother, and shouldst lay me to rest in thy city, then of a surety wilt thou be glorified above all other princes in the land, and thy sons and grandsons also, and this city will itself be glorified above other Russian towns, and the Saints will come and dwell in it, and its hands will prevail against its enemies. Thus will it ever be as long as my bones lie therein.

Many Russians came to believe in the authenticity of the incident because two years after Peter's death Metropolitan Theognost suddenly decided to settle in Moscow. From that time the spiritual and secular authorities worked in close harmony, a development crucial to Moscow's rise to preeminence in Russia.

The prophesy gained further credibility as Ivan undertook to fulfill its stipulation that additional churches be constructed in the Kremlin. Before Peter's death, he and Ivan had jointly laid the foundation stone of the Cathedral of the Assumption (Uspenski sobor), after which the leader of the Russian Church "with his own hands built a stone grave for himself in the wall." Ivan was moved by religious piety to sponsor this enterprise, but he plainly also had political considerations in mind. If his principality was to play a major role in Russian affairs, it would have to be graced with a more

elegant and imposing capital. As a grand prince — and as the khan's tax collector — he had occasion to call princely congresses, but none of the existing structures was suitable for such meetings. Moreover, Ivan felt obliged to put a stately house of worship at the disposal of the high Church dignitaries who frequently visited the metropolitan at the Kremlin.

To dramatize the growing power and grandeur of his principality, Ivan ordered that stone, rather than wood, be used in the construction of the new churches. Between 1328 and 1333 three of these imposing stone structures were completed: the Cathedral of the Assumption, in which the metropolitans were buried; the Church of Ioann Lestvichnik; and the Cathedral of the Archangel Michael, burial place of the Muscovite princes. A fourth, the Church of the Savior in the Forest (Spas na bory), a monastery and center of learning, was constructed of wood. Ivan generously supplied the monks in this last church with funds for books and food and granted them certain legal privileges and immunities. (The wooden frame of the Church of the Savior in the Forest has been preserved as a national relic and now stands in the inner court of the Grand Kremlin Palace.) It is noteworthy that at this time only three other cities in all of Russia — Novgorod, Pskov, and Tver — could boast of stone buildings. By the simple, if expensive, device of encouraging the use of stone Ivan saw to it that the expansion of the Kremlin attracted attention all over the country.

While implementing his ambitious plans Ivan suffered some cruel setbacks. As was to happen with distressing frequency, fires broke out in 1331 and 1337. Since practically all the buildings still were wooden,

the flames spread quickly and destroyed a large section of the Kremlin. Two years after the second fire, the indomitable Kalita began to rebuild. Taking no chances, he had the fragile pine walls replaced with the toughest wood available — huge oak timbers some fifty feet long and twenty-eight inches thick. In a year's time the Kremlin was both enlarged and restored. Kalita enjoyed his new fortress only briefly, however, for he died in 1340.

Ironically, Ivan's policy of accommodation to the Tatars, so degrading to many of his countrymen, ultimately made it possible for Moscow to assume leadership in the struggle against the oppressors. Even the two natural catastrophes that befell the city in the middle of the fourteenth century at most only delayed that development. In 1353 the bubonic plague that had taken the lives of a quarter of the population of Western Europe reached Moscow and struck down many of its citizens, including Prince Simeon the Proud, Ivan's disciple and successor, and Metropolitan Theognost. Twelve years later, the most devastating fire to date — the so-called Great Fire — consumed much of the Kremlin. But by this time Muscovy, the strongest principality in northeast Russia, was able to recover rapidly from such disasters. Still, when Kalita's grandson Dmitri assumed the title of grand prince in 1359, Muscovy was not yet a match for the Golden Horde, a deficiency that the talented and courageous young ruler determined to rectify.

Before challenging the Tatars, however, Dmitri prudently set about fortifying the Kremlin, which in any case he considered too small a capital for his expanding realm. He had the wooden stockade torn down and the

fortress enlarged. For the new wall — which took fifteen years to build — wood was abandoned in favor of white stone especially imported from Miachkov, some fifteen miles from Moscow. Dmitri's bold enterprise evoked respectful comment throughout Russia, for not even the prominent and wealthy city of Tver was encircled by a stone wall.

Dmitri scored his first military victories in the 1360's and early 1370's, when he fended off the combined attacks of Lithuania and Tver. Flushed with these successes, he began to defy the Tatars by refusing to pay the usual annual tribute. In 1378 he added insult to injury by defeating the Mongols in a minor battle near the Vozh River. This enraged the proud Khan Mamai, who realized that if he did not subdue the rebellious Dmitri, Mongol authority all over Russia would evaporate. Mamai organized a huge army and in 1380, after forming an alliance with Lithuania, crossed the Volga and advanced toward Moscow.

In an attempt to settle the issue without bloodshed, Mamai offered Dmitri peace in return for the resumption of tribute in the amount customary before 1371. The grand prince responded by appealing to other Russian princes to join him in a crusade against the Tatars. Several answered the call and by the summer of 1380 he had assembled an army of 30,000 men, mostly from his own principality. Khan Mamai's army was roughly the same size, but he enjoyed the advantage of superior cavalry forces.

On September 8 the two armies stood poised for battle on Kulikovo pole (Snipes Field), a plain between the upper Don and its tributary, the Nepriadva. In accordance with the traditions of steppe warfare, before the fighting began one of the Tatars challenged the Russians to a duel. A monk accompanying Dmitri's army accepted the challenge and galloped full speed toward his opponent. They collided with such tremendous force that both died on the spot. Minutes later, the two huge armies lunged at each other along a seven-mile front.

For four hours Mamai's cavalry relentlessly assailed the Muscovite army, which was on the verge of total collapse. But Dmitri had cleverly held a large detachment of his best troops in ambush in a nearby forest, and just when all seemed lost, he called on his reserves. The sudden appearance of fresh troops not only breathed new life into the Muscovite army but demoralized the Tatars. The tide of battle turned completely: Mamai abruptly fled, his army disintegrated, and Prince Dmitri captured the Tatar camp along with large quantities of booty. The Russian force had lost about one half of its men, including the commander in chief and several other ranking officers. Nonetheless, it was a superb victory — and the first time that a large Mongol army had been routed by Russians in a major test of strength. In the nineteenth century one historian interpreted it as nothing less than "a sign of the triumph of Europe over Asia."

In the wake of the battle Grand Prince Dmitri's stature rose immeasurably in Russia, not only by virtue of his victory but also because of his personal bravery. "He was the first in battle," notes a contemporary account of the conflict, "and killed many Tatars." At one point he singlehandedly took on four Mongol attackers and was knocked unconscious. At the end of the battle his officers found him under a pile of dead

Dmitri Donskoi's decision to replace Ivan Kalita's wooden stockade (near right) with white stone battlements (far right) was both politically and architecturally innovative. The imposing new citadel, unique in all of Russia, was not only fireproof but virtually impregnable to Tatar attack.

bodies. His armor was slashed to pieces, but he was only slightly wounded and capable of resuming command.

Grand Prince Dmitri fully understood the symbolic and political significance of his victory, and he therefore went to great lengths to publicize it. On his return from Kulikovo pole he led a triumphant procession into the Kremlin. He entered the Cathedral of the Archangel Michael and, standing solemnly before the coffins of his forefathers, gave thanks to God for his victory. He then proceeded to the Cathedral of the Assumption and repeated the ritual. The church dignitaries decreed that the Saturday on or before October 26 (the day of Saint Dmitri of Salonike, the grand prince's patron saint) was to be observed as a memorial day "as long as Russia exists."

But the Muscovites were not able to rejoice for long. In 1382 Mamai's successor, Khan Tokhtamysh, prepared to avenge the defeat and reassert Tatar authority. With amazing speed and secrecy he led a large army composed entirely of cavalry into northeastern Russia. Only when Tokhtamysh crossed the middle Volga did the Russian princes sense the gravity of their situation. Terrified, the grand princes of Riazan and Suzdal announced their neutrality and even promised to help the invader. Caught off guard, Dmitri fled to the north to organize a new army. He apparently believed that the Kremlin's stone walls could withstand any Tatar siege, and that some recently acquired firearms would enable the Muscovites to hold the enemy at bay until he could return with a relief force.

No sooner had the prince departed than pandemonium broke loose in the fortress. The wealthy citizens wanted to preserve themselves by quitting the city, but the commoners demanded that everyone remain to help strengthen the defenses against the impending attack. When the well-to-do Muscovites persisted with their escape plans, civil disorder erupted. Many of the offenders were killed, and their property was looted as commoners seized control of the city. Distrusting the local nobility, the rebellious peasants chose a Lithuanian visitor, Prince Ostei, to command the garrison.

For the next few days the Muscovites engaged in feverish preparations. They brought in supplies, burned down many of the surrounding settlements and trees to give them a clearer view of the advancing enemy, and offered shelter to thousands of people living in the environs. By the time Tokhtamysh's army had encamped nearby and laid siege to the Kremlin, the defenders were supremely confident both of its impregnability and of their military prowess. Several Muscovites climbed to the top of the fortress and taunted the Tatars, who were taken aback by the audacity of their foes. For three days and nights the Mongols furiously attacked the Kremlin, but each time they were repulsed and suffered heavy losses.

Had Tokhtamysh not resorted to cruel deception, the defenders would probably have forced the enemy to retreat. But on the fourth day the khan sent a message to the Kremlin abjuring any intention of causing harm and requesting merely some "small gifts" and an opportunity to visit the city. Naïvely, the Muscovites opened the gates to the Kremlin and dispatched a religious procession, led by Prince Ostei, to greet Tokhtamysh and offer him presents. As soon as the last members of the group cleared the Kremlin gates, the khan's

henchmen pounced on the stunned and defenseless Muscovites, killing the prince and many of his companions. Other Mongols rushed through the open gates or climbed over the walls on ladders that had been held in readiness for the attack.

The next few hours were ghastly. A flash fire spread through the Kremlin, and those who managed to escape the flames were cut down by Mongol swords. Everywhere "there was grief and sobbing, and loud howling, and tears, and inconsolable cries, and much groaning." When the killing and looting finally stopped, the Kremlin was a shambles. Ten thousand bodies were found, but it is known that many more people lost their lives during the carnage. "Until then," the chronicler lamented, "the city of Moscow had been large and wonderful to look at, crowded as she was with people, filled with wealth and glory . . . and now all at once her beauty perished and her glory disappeared. Nothing could be seen but smoking ruins and bare earth and heaps of corpses."

It appeared that with this blow Tokhtamysh had fully restored the supremacy of the Golden Horde over Moscow and, indeed, over all of Russia. But in reality the Mongol empire was in no position to exploit the victory of 1382, for as a result of endless internecine struggles between rival khans, the empire was slowly disintegrating. The Tatars could still cause considerable devastation on occasion, as they did when they looted the countryside around Moscow in 1408–9. But they could no longer mount a successful siege against the reconstructed Kremlin, for any forays they did undertake were nothing more than isolated displays of momentary — and perpetually waning — strength.

Had Muscovy not been weakened by a fierce dynastic feud, it is conceivable that the Russians might have shortened the Tatar rule by fifty years. But when Grand Prince Vasili I died in 1425, he bequeathed his throne not to his brother Iuri, who followed him in seniority, but to his son Vasili II, who was then only ten years old. Iuri, claiming to be the rightful heir, declared war against Moscow — and so began the first and only military conflict between descendants of Ivan Kalita.

For some twenty-five years the two factions fought for control of the Kremlin. The struggle became particularly brutal after Iuri's death in 1434, when his sons, Vasili the Squint-Eyed and Dmitri Shemiaka, assumed command of the forces allied against Vasili II. In one of these clashes Vasili II captured his cousin Vasili the Squint-Eyed and viciously blinded him. The custom of blinding pretenders to the throne was widely practiced in Byzantium, but in Russia this form of torture had been used only once before (in the twelfth century), and consequently it shocked many Russians. In fact, Vasili II himself eventually came to regret it, for in 1446 Dmitri Shemiaka captured Vasili II and ordered that he be similarly blinded. As soon as Vasili II — now known as "Vasili the Dark" — was released, he led a new revolt against his rivals. By 1452 he had crushed them once and for all: Shemiaka fled to Novgorod, where he was poisoned by a Muscovite agent, and Vasili the Squint-Eyed also met a violent end. It is not known whether Grand Prince Vasili II had a hand in the murder of his cousins, but when apprised of their deaths he displayed "indecent joy."

Although now blind, Vasili II lived up to his father's

иполашо́пих҃ . достіхнил́ остѧ́кни даꙗль п҃
исолеꙗблетсѧ а шоломы на главаꙗ и хꙋ ани оу тренꙗ а з
ра с вꙗтꙗ цисаꙗ во времꙗ авера елоꙗбцы шоломоꙗй нꙗплꙗмеꙗ́й
гнены и полеꙗблꙗсѧ

In a virtuoso display of both personal courage and tactical genius, Dmitri Donskoi dealt Khan Mamai and his Tatar warriors a staggering blow at Kulikovo pole in 1380. In a clash that one historian was to label "a sign of the triumph of Europe over Asia," the Muscovite forces ended almost 250 years of Mongol rule. This leaf from a contemporary manuscript shows Dmitri and his brother reviewing their troops from a hilltop. At right, the brothers give thanks to the Savior for their stunning military victory.

expectations. He substantially expanded the boundaries of Muscovy, and by the time he died in 1462 the principality comprised some 15,000 square miles. It was now twenty-five times as large as it had been at the time of Ivan Kalita, some 150 years earlier. Although Vasili formally recognized the Tatars as the supreme authority in Russia, he delivered only a small portion of the customary tribute, and this he did not pay regularly. The Tatars were no longer able to challenge him, and as a result most of the tribute that Vasili collected enriched his own treasury. Three hundred years had elapsed since Moscow had been founded, and in that time the Kremlin had become the seat of a major state that enjoyed virtual independence.

But Moscow did not owe its preeminence in Russia solely to its accretion of material power. Its religious importance was further enhanced in the fifteenth century when it replaced Constantinople as the spiritual center of the Greek Orthodox Church. In 1439 the patriarch in Byzantium proclaimed religious unity between Orthodoxy and Roman Catholicism in order to gain Western help against the advancing Turks. The Muscovites refused to accept the "heretical" union, and they unceremoniously confined their own metropolitan, Isidor, to the Chudov Monastery in the Kremlin for having dared to invoke the pope's name while celebrating a solemn mass in the Cathedral of the Assumption. A few years later the Russian bishops, strongly encouraged by Vasili II, elected Bishop Iona of Riazan as the Metropolitan of the Russian Church. They did this without even consulting the patriarch in Constantinople.

Moscow's spiritual independence became final in 1453, when Constantinople fell into the hands of the infidel Turks, an event that Russians came to regard as just punishment for Byzantium's heretical dealings with Rome. Within a few decades a Russian monk named Filofei was able to contend that both Rome and Constantinople had lost their standing in the spiritual world by abandoning the true faith. "Two Romes have fallen," he asserted, "and the third stands, and a fourth shall not be." Moscow, of course, was the "Third Rome," entitled to moral supremacy in Christendom and destined for eternal life because only there had heresy been shunned. The rulers in the Kremlin naturally seized on Filofei's doctrine to bolster their claims to political leadership in Russia. And this in part explains why after the middle of the fifteenth century the history of the whole country increasingly turned on events in the Muscovite principality.

II
The Third Rome

On November 12, 1472, crowds of Muscovites lined the snow-covered streets of the Kremlin to catch a glimpse of the Byzantine princess Zoë Palaeologa, who had come all the way from Rome to marry Grand Prince Ivan III. Many people were dismayed by the thought of a "Roman" first lady, but this did not dampen anyone's curiosity. The grand prince himself must have been torn between anticipation and apprehension that day, for he had never set eyes on his bride. It was too late for second thoughts, however; the marriage contract had already been signed in Rome by Gian-Battista della Volpe, Ivan's Italian Master of the Mint, who had acted as the prince's proxy.

On the day of Zoë's arrival a solemn mass was performed, and it was immediately followed by the wedding ceremony itself. Metropolitan Philip of Moscow presided over the affair, which was held in a makeshift structure used during the rebuilding of the Cathedral of the Assumption. To mark her conversion from Roman Catholicism to Greek Orthodoxy the metropolitan changed Zoë's name to Sofia.

To the civilized world, the exotic union between a Muscovite grand prince and a member of the imperial family of Byzantium seemed to portend far-reaching political changes on the international scene. The two principal actors in the drama did not attach the same cosmic significance to it, however. To Ivan, marriage to a Byzantine princess symbolized increased status as a ruler within Russia itself. To Zoë, the move to Moscow offered escape from the poverty and humiliation she had recently suffered in Rome. In short, both partners looked upon the arrangement as a marriage of convenience.

Almost from the time of her birth in 1448, Zoë had been deprived of the pleasures and perquisites normally associated with persons of her background. When she was five years old, her uncle Emperor Constantine XI was killed fighting the Turks, who then captured Constantinople. Shortly thereafter her father, Thomas Palaeologus, fled to Italy with his wife and three children. In 1462 both parents died unexpectedly. Fortunately for Zoë and her siblings, the elder Palaeologi had taken the precaution of entrusting the youngsters' care to Pope Paul II. Unfortunately for them, the pope made the mistake of charging the heavy-handed Cardinal Bessarion with their upbringing.

A Greek scholar of some note and a convert to Roman Catholicism, Bessarion could effectively impart religious training, but his competence as a foster parent left much to be desired. Not for one moment did he allow Zoë and her brothers to forget that they were orphans, refugees, and paupers. Time and again he urged them not to boast of their royal origins and to demonstrate their gratitude to their benefactor.

Bessarion's constant reminders thoroughly dispirited the princess, and her oldest brother, Andrew, heir to the Byzantine throne, reacted even more negatively to the harsh admonitions of the cardinal. He grew up to be a frivolous man whose extravagant life style always exceeded his means. He is known to have sold his right to the throne on three separate occasions. Still, Zoë's stay in Rome was not without its rewards. It exposed her to the most sophisticated culture of the period and endowed her with an excellent education. By the time she left for Moscow she had mastered Latin and Italian in addition to her native Greek.

Beyond this, Zoë is a somewhat shadowy and controversial figure. Not a single reliable record of her features survives; even the portrait that was sent to Ivan in 1470 has disappeared. The Italian princess Clarissa Orsini, who visited Zoë in Rome in 1472, described her as beautiful, but the Florentine poet Luigi Pulci, who was present at the same meeting, claimed that she was repulsively fat. According to yet another report, she weighed well over three hundred pounds.

More important, there are conflicting views about Zoë's influence over Ivan III. One sixteenth-century writer characterized her as a "Greek sorceress," responsible not only for Ivan's blunders but also for the poisoning of her husband's son by a previous marriage. Most modern historians doubt that she exercised marked influence on Ivan's political program, but there is little question that she had a hand in promoting the remodeling of the Kremlin, which in the course of her stay was transformed into an architectural center unrivaled in all of Russia for its beauty and diversity.

No one knows who took the initiative in arranging the match between Zoë and Ivan, but her guardian, Paul II, seems the most likely candidate. He probably hoped that Zoë's presence in Moscow would strengthen Roman Catholic influence in Russia and thus help him to secure Ivan's support for a crusade against the Ottoman Turks, who were pushing their way into southeastern Europe. But the pope was to be disappointed on both scores; Ivan had his own reasons for favoring the marriage — and they had nothing to do with papal interests.

Ivan III, known as Ivan the Great, was one of Muscovy's ablest and most ambitious rulers. Thoroughly trained in the arts of government and war, he ascended the throne in 1462 at the age of twenty-two and immediately revealed his intention to centralize authority and consolidate all of Russia under his domination. He firmly believed that his power derived directly from God, and when Holy Roman Emperor Frederick III offered him the title of King of Russia, Ivan responded with more than a trace of arrogance:

> We by the grace of God have been sovereigns over our dominions from the beginning, from our first forebears, and our right we hold from God, as did our forebears. We pray to God that it may be granted to us and our children for all time to continue as sovereigns as we are at present, and as in the past we have never needed appointment from anyone, so now we do not desire it.

Despite the prince's exalted opinion of his status — and despite his aggressive foreign and domestic policies — he was never reckless. He weighed his chances carefully and whenever possible tried to achieve his aims through diplomacy rather than war. Military glory for its own sake meant little to Ivan. In fact, he rarely accompanied his armies on their campaigns, preferring to remain in his Kremlin palace and plan his involved diplomatic moves. Once he decided on military action, however, he generally pursued it to the end.

Nothing illustrates this latter trait more clearly than Ivan's dealings with Lithuania. In 1495 he arranged for the marriage of his daughter Elena to Grand Prince Alexander of Lithuania, a Roman Catholic. He craftily inserted into the marriage contract the stipulation that Elena be permitted to practice the Orthodox religion without restraint. Five years later, on the spurious pre-

Under Ivan III (right), the strong-featured tsar whose forceful personality was to shape Muscovy's destiny for four crucial decades, the Kremlin became the political nexus of northwestern Russia. In the years following his marriage to Byzantine princess Zoë Palaeologa, Ivan the Great annexed half a dozen neighboring territories, permanently eliminated the Tatar threat, and added a series of splendid new buildings to the Kremlin compound. The contemporary map below shows the refurbished Kremlin as it looked at the end of Ivan's reign. At that time the white stone churches that are the tsar's architectural legacy were still surrounded by private homes.

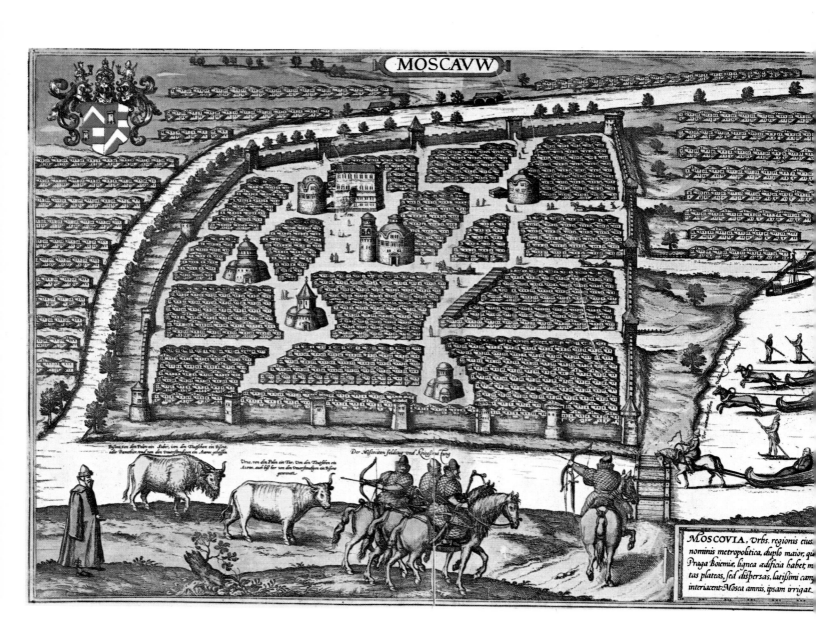

text that Alexander had violated the agreement by exerting pressure on Elena to convert, he attacked Lithuania and seized extensive territory. Elena pleaded with her father to halt the campaign against her husband. "He allows me to maintain my faith according to the Greek custom," she declared, "to go from one holy church to another, and to have at my court priests, deacons and choristers." Although distressed by this exposure of the hypocrisy of his policy, Ivan refused to yield. Instead he rebuked Elena and warned that she would suffer eternal damnation for her failure to uphold Orthodoxy.

Despite the fact that he obviously valued state interests above family ties, Ivan was not an especially cruel or heartless man by the standards of his time. He subdued those who opposed him but he derived no pleasure from tormenting his adversaries. His cold and calculating approach to affairs of state did not endear him to many people. Yet there were few who did not respect him for his impressive achievements.

Ivan had acted with characteristic caution when Pope Paul II offered him Zoë Palaeologa's hand in 1469. It may be that his initial reluctance stemmed from a reverence for his first wife, Princess Maria of Tver, who had died in 1467. Ivan had married her when he was twelve years old, and he seems to have been devoted to her. She had borne him only one son, however, and Ivan did not consider a single heir sufficient to guarantee the succession. The prince felt compelled to remarry, and after a suitable period of mourning, he began searching for a second wife. Following three years of negotiations, Ivan settled on Zoë. He felt that marriage to her would confirm his supremacy over the boyars in his principality. His predecessors had all married Russian or Lithuanian princesses, and Ivan, who had drastically reduced the political power of the aristocracy, was eager to demonstrate that his elevated position enabled him to choose a bride who not only came from outside the realm but who also came from one of the most distinguished royal families in the world.

At the very last moment a crisis occurred that almost prevented the marriage from taking place. Zoë was traveling with a large company of friends and attendants, among them Cardinal Antonio Bonumbre, who committed the indiscretion of publicly displaying the "Latin cross." Nothing could have offended the religious sensibilities of the Orthodox Russians more deeply. Metropolitan Philip announced that he would leave the city if the cardinal were permitted to desecrate the Kremlin with the crucifix, and Ivan immediately dispatched a messenger to Bonumbre with a warning not to uncover the crucifix in the capital. The cardinal, conscious of the pope's interest in the marriage, yielded, and Zoë, rebaptized Sofia, became Grand Princess of Muscovy.

Sofia had no reason to regret her move to the Kremlin. Although she endured some trying moments, her thirty-one years as the sovereign's wife were both exciting and rewarding. For one thing, she witnessed the enormous expansion of the power and territory of the Muscovite state. Even before her arrival, Ivan had set in motion the first phase of his plan to become the national sovereign by adding Yaroslavl to his holdings. Thereafter he continued the "gathering of the Russian land" by extending his control over Novgorod, Perm, Tver, Viatka, Viazma, and certain lands held by

Lithuania. But the single most dramatic event of his reign was the final collapse of the Tatar domination over Russia.

According to a popular legend, Khan Ahmed demanded that Ivan resume paying the customary tribute to the Golden Horde in 1480. When the Tatar emissary appeared, Ivan is said to have defiantly spat upon the khan's badge of authority without suffering punishment. This legend seems to have been invented in order to preserve the reputation of the grand prince, who hardly distinguished himself for bravery during the crisis. The punitive force sent by the khan met the Muscovite army on the banks of the Ugra River in 1480. As the troops prepared for battle, Ivan abruptly lost his nerve and abandoned them. The amazed and utterly dismayed citizens of Moscow then received a second shock: Khan Ahmed also panicked and withdrew his army. Thus the vaunted Tatar yoke that had bound Russia for almost two and a half centuries dissolved without the firing of a shot.

The prestige that Muscovy acquired as a result of its independence and territorial growth was reflected in diverse ways. Ivan began referring to himself with increasing frequency as "Tsar of All Rus" and "Autocrat," by which he meant to suggest not so much that he exercised unlimited authority within his realm as that he was independent of all foreigners. Court etiquette and ceremonials became ever more elaborate, and beginning in the 1490's the Byzantine crest of the double eagle was affixed to all state documents. In this way Ivan gave currency to the notion that his marriage to Sofia had conferred upon him the position of logical successor to the Byzantine emperors. The double eagle remained the official crest of tsarist Russia until the Revolution of 1917.

One of the most striking signs of Muscovy's growing importance was the magnificent rebuilding of the Kremlin. The series of fires that raged through the citadel in 1468 and 1469 made it necessary for Ivan to restore the capital; his decision to do so on a grand scale resulted at least in part from a desire to please Sofia. She found it depressing to live in the inelegant city of Moscow. Its small wooden houses, rows of identical shops, and modest fortress surrounded by shabby walls were a far cry from the splendors of Constantinople and Rome. Ivan also realized that a more comfortable and appealing setting would impress the increasing number of foreign diplomats and merchants arriving at his capital.

For the first time in Muscovy's history a grand prince invited Western architects and engineers to work on the Kremlin. Once again Sofia's influence seems to have been instrumental, but there was another more pragmatic reason for the bold innovation. In 1471 two master builders from Moscow, Mishkin and Kristov, had begun to lay the foundations for a new Cathedral of the Assumption. During the earthquake that struck Moscow a year later, portions of the new walls collapsed — chiefly because they had been poorly constructed. Ivan then hired several Pskov masons who were familiar with Western building techniques, but they too proved unequal to the task.

The grand prince concluded that the requisite skills could only be found abroad, and so he sent the boyar Simeon Tolbuzin to Italy to engage the most gifted architects there. One chronicler reports that in Venice

Determined to create a capital worthy of the growing power and prominence of the Muscovite state, Ivan the Great commissioned native architects to erect a new Cathedral of the Assumption inside the Kremlin's walls. When the half-finished structure collapsed in 1472, the frustrated tsar recruited foreigners to complete the task. Led by Aristotele Fieraventi, a small band of Italian artisans constructed a new cathedral (below right) that achieved a striking synthesis of Russian architectural forms and Western building techniques. Inspired by Fieraventi's model, architects from Pskov began work on the Cathedral of the Annunciation (below left) four years later.

Tolbuzin accidentally encountered a leading master, Aristotele Fieraventi, who was also a talented magician. Fieraventi dazzled Tolbuzin by pouring first water and then wine and honey from an empty pewter vessel into a copper dish. In fact, "whatever was requested, began to flow." The credulous citizens of Moscow believed this tale and regarded Fieraventi as a mysterious man possessed of fabulous powers.

Actually Tolbuzin's meeting with Fieraventi was probably planned on the advice of Sofia herself, who must have been familiar with the work of the renowned artist. Born around 1415 into a family of architects, Aristotele received superb training, and early in life he carved out a remarkable career for himself. By the 1450's he excelled not only in architecture but also in engineering, the casting of cannon and bells, and the minting of money. In 1453 he was appointed engineer to the city of Bologna, and thereafter he frequently worked in other cities on special projects. In 1467, for example, he journeyed to Hungary to build a bridge across the Danube for King Matthias Corvinus.

Normally an Italian master who was as successful as Fieraventi would not have been attracted to Moscow, which Westerners looked upon as a half-savage, bitterly cold outpost. Indeed, before Tolbuzin's arrival Fieraventi had rejected an invitation to work for the sultan in Constantinople because of the many stories he had heard about the barbarity of the Moslem ruler. But in 1473, while temporarily employed in Rome, Aristotele had been maliciously slandered. Several rival masters, spreading the rumor that he had forged coins, succeeded in discrediting him. He eventually proved that the charges were baseless, but only after he had been im-

prisoned and dismissed from his post in Bologna. Consequently Tolbuzin's offer of a position at Ivan's court and a generous salary of ten rubles a month caught Aristotele at an opportune moment. Early in 1475 Fieraventi, his son Andrea, and an apprentice named Pietro joined the Russian envoy on the long trip to Moscow. It marked the beginning of a new and productive career for the sixty-year-old master — and a new era in Kremlin architecture as well.

Fieraventi immediately set to work on the Uspenski sobor, or Cathedral of the Assumption. Ivan did not want an entirely foreign structure, but rather a church modeled generally after the Uspenski sobor in Vladimir. The Venetian visited that ancient city, as well as several others, and then tried to synthesize the dynastic and spiritual traditions of Russia with the most advanced building techniques of Western Europe. The result was a grandiose and majestic church that eclipsed the Vladimir cathedral in splendor and beauty. Architecturally, the most obvious difference between the two structures is that the Moscow cathedral has six piers instead of the usual four, which lengthened the square shape into an oblong. Fieraventi also erected five apses in place of the traditional three, and by eliminating the galleries he succeeded in creating a spaciousness hitherto unknown in any Russian building. Finally, in order to enhance the solidity of the cathedral, he built deep, oversized foundations on which he placed walls of white stone. It took Fieraventi four summers to complete this first "truly Renaissance building in Russian dress."

Ivan could not have been more delighted. At last his capital could boast of at least one showplace that did not suffer by comparison with those of Rome, Venice, and Constantinople. The grand prince celebrated the cathedral's completion by inviting the leading Church dignitaries, the boyars, and his personal retainers to a sumptuous dinner. Several ecclesiastics remained in the palace as his guests for an entire week. In addition, Ivan bestowed lavish gifts on monasteries, monks, and priests in the Moscow region as well as on the Italian master himself. This largesse notwithstanding, Ivan cannot be accused of squandering money on the cathedral. Although some restorative work has been necessary, it is still one of the most engaging sights in the Kremlin.

In the fall of 1479 the Bologna authorities invited Fieraventi to return to his former post, claiming that only he could be entrusted with the remodeling of the palace of the Podesta. The appeal stunned Ivan, for he had come to rely heavily on the Italian master. In the winter of 1477–78, for example, Fieraventi had accompanied the grand prince on a campaign against Novgorod. In his capacity as military engineer and supervisor of artillery, the Venetian had constructed a bridge across the Volkhov River that had greatly aided the advance of the Muscovite army. Small wonder, then, that Ivan simply refused to let Fieraventi return to his native land. During the six years preceding his death in 1485, the Italian trained a corps of Russian blacksmiths in the manufacture of cannon, while working simultaneously as a sculptor and minter. Never again was Russia to enjoy the services of a man gifted in so many fields of technical knowledge.

Despite his diverse talents and prodigious energy, Fieraventi could not undertake to redesign the Kremlin by himself. And Ivan, who felt that he could entrust only one major building, the Cathedral of the Annunciation, to Russian architects, was obliged to turn once again to Italy for assistance. He managed to attract several accomplished masters to his capital, and in the course of twenty years they thoroughly transformed the ancient fortress. In 1487 Marco Ruffo laid the foundation of the Palace on the Quay, and at about the same time he and Pietro Solario began to build the Palace of Facets (Granovitaia palata), so-called because of its patterned façade. Completed in four years, that simple stone structure resembles several early Renaissance palaces in Italy, especially the Palazzo Bevilacqua and the Palazzo dei Diamanti in Ferrara. Future tsars were to preside over state banquets from the throne room, a large, vaulted hall on the second story, and it was there that foreign ambassadors were received and major military victories celebrated. The hall comprises an area seventy feet by seventy-seven feet, and it gives the appearance of being even more spacious because of a massive pier in the center that made it possible to place four cross vaults across the room.

A few months before his death in 1505, Ivan commissioned Alevisio Novi to rebuild the Cathedral of the Archangel Michael, which, like the Cathedral of the Assumption, was to be modeled after the Vladimir Uspenski sobor. Alevisio remained more faithful to the original than Fieraventi had been, but even he introduced some noteworthy changes. Among other things, he covered the walls with Renaissance features: arches, pilasters, panels, and sculptural details. As a result the exterior has much in common with the palaces that characterize the Italian High Renaissance.

From 1499 to 1508 Alevisio built new living quarters for the royal family at the top of Kremlin Hill. The construction of the imposing Terem Palace (Teremnoi dvorets) was prompted not merely by a desire for greater comfort and luxury — the tsar's previous quarters had been destroyed in 1493 by the Kremlin's perennial leveler, fire. For a time Ivan had actually lived in a peasant house near the Iauza River. As the royal residence neared completion, several of Moscow's outstanding citizens also built private homes within the confines of the Kremlin.

Ivan was understandably eager to provide maximum protection for this splendid array of churches and palaces. The once-famous Kremlin wall had fallen into decay. Moreover, it suffered from an intolerable weakness: certain portions had never been rebuilt in stone and at these very points a Tatar force had penetrated the fortress in 1451. To remedy this situation Ivan charged Solario and Ruffo in 1485 with the erection of an entirely new wall, a task that occupied them for no less than ten years' time. Even then, neither the towers nor the ornamental decorations were completed. The snail-like pace of construction stemmed from fear of an enemy attack, which prevented the architects from removing more than a small portion of the old bulwark at any one time.

In tackling their assignment, the Italians broke with tradition in a number of ways. First of all, they substituted red brick for the white stone used 120 years earlier. In addition, to make breaching the new fortifications more difficult, they erected a double — and, at some points, triple — system of walls separated by moats. Ivan went to the trouble of engaging another Italian, Aloisio de Carcano, a distinguished hydraulic engineer, to excavate for the moats. No reproductions of these walls are extant, but from contemporary accounts it appears that they resembled those surrounding fortresses in northern Italy, particularly in Milan and Ferrara.

By the 1490's the Grand Princess Sofia must have felt thoroughly at home in the Kremlin, which was being gradually transformed into a citadel worthy of Byzantine royalty. Sofia was far from content, however, for the future of her children, especially her eldest son, Vasili, was not secure. She had always hoped that Vasili would succeed Ivan on the throne; and when Ivan Molodoi, the grand prince's only son by his first wife, died unexpectedly in 1490, Vasili seemed the most likely successor. But seven years earlier Ivan Molodoi's wife, Elena Stepanovna, had given birth to a son, Dmitri. Never before in Muscovy's history had the question of the succession presented itself in quite this fashion. Who was the rightful heir to the throne: Dmitri, the ruler's grandson by his first wife, or Vasili, his son by his second wife? In the absence of precedent only Ivan III himself could decide.

Unfortunately for the grand prince, both claimants were represented by their mothers, ambitious and skillful intriguers. Moreover, there existed between the women a long history of mutual antagonism, and therefore neither was inclined to be magnanimous toward the other. From the moment Elena married Ivan Molodoi and moved into the Kremlin, Sofia had eyed her stepson's wife with suspicion. She seems to have sensed that someday their children would be rival claimants for the Russian throne.

Then in 1483, the year Dmitri was born, a nasty incident shattered all hopes for cordial relations between them. Overjoyed at the birth of a grandson, Ivan decided to present Elena with some jewels from his first wife's dowry. But he had already entrusted them to Sofia, and she in turn had given some to her impecunious brother Andrew and a few others to Andrew's daughter on the occasion of her wedding. On learning this, Ivan flew into a rage and tried to retrieve the gems by force, apparently without success. From that time on Sofia harbored nothing but ill will toward Elena, who had been the unwitting cause of Ivan's tactless behavior. The grand princess seems to have held her animosity in check for fourteen years. Then in 1497 the first of a series of conflicts erupted that would determine the fate of Ivan the Great's crown.

In the summer of 1497 Vasili somehow discovered that Ivan intended to appoint his grandson "Grand Prince of Vladimir and Moscow." To forestall the move, Sofia and several boyars — who saw a chance to regain some of the power they had lost to Ivan — hatched an elaborate conspiracy. They planned to seize the treasury, set up an authority openly in rebellion against Ivan, and place Vasili at its head. Sofia was rumored to be trafficking with "evil women" who were supplying her with poison for Dmitri and possibly even for Ivan himself. But before the plan could be executed, the conspirators were discovered. Ivan immediately placed Vasili under house arrest, disgraced Sofia, and ordered the execution of a number of the "evil women." "From that time on," the chronicler tells us, Ivan "began to live with . . . [Sofia] in great vigilance." The boyar conspirators were quickly tried and found guilty; six were beheaded on the ice of the Moscow River and many others were imprisoned.

A few weeks later Ivan conducted an elaborate ceremony in the Kremlin's Cathedral of the Assumption, during which he crowned Dmitri his co-grand prince. Standing in front of three thrones — one for himself, one for Dmitri, and one for the Metropolitan Simon — Ivan explained that he was following the ancient custom of appointing as his successor the male offspring of his first son. Thereupon the metropolitan, his hand on Dmitri's head, read the prayer of appointment and blessed the regalia: the *shapka,* a cap of gold and carnelians, and the *barmi,* a broad collar of pearls. Ivan himself arranged the bejeweled symbols of office on his grandson's head and shoulders. After the Te Deum, Ivan concluded the ceremony with an appeal to Dmitri to rule justly, love God, and protect Orthodoxy. Then the assembled guests were treated to a final spectacle: the showering of the heir apparent with gold and silver coins in front of the Kremlin's three major cathedrals.

A less resourceful person than Sofia might have acknowledged defeat at this point and given up the struggle. But adversity only whetted her appetite for intrigue. She had the story spread that Vasili had been the innocent victim of the nefarious boyars who had engineered the trial of the conspirators of 1497. At first the shrewd Sofia did not make these charges herself but saw to it that respected men at court uttered them. Soon it was widely believed that Ivan had turned against his wife and son under the influence of "the Devil's sorcery and the advice of evil men." The intrigue had the desired effect on the grand prince, who

Ivan the Great's talented son and successor, Vasili III (right), had ruled Moscow for more than a decade when Baron Sigismund von Herberstein arrived in the Russian capital in 1517 to assume his post as the Holy Roman Empire's ambassador to the tsar's court. Fascinated and somewhat repelled by what he found, Herberstein compiled the first detailed commentary on Russian life. His frank and engrossing report, published in Vienna in 1550, was illustrated with woodcuts of Tatar warriors (far left), snow-covered steppes (left), and other typically Russian scenes.

began "to drink so much at dinner that he was overcome with sleep. In the meantime all those invited were frightened and silent." Convinced by 1499 that he had indeed been duped, Ivan ordered the arrest of numerous boyars who had opposed Vasili. One was beheaded on the ice of the Moscow River and several others were committed to a monastery. Ivan completed this astonishing reversal by restoring Sofia to favor and naming Vasili Grand Prince of Novgorod and Pskov.

Vasili's victory was only partial, however, for his rival retained the title of Grand Prince of Vladimir and Moscow. But Sofia and her son continued their campaign of intrigue, and in 1502 Ivan completed the undoing of Dmitri and Elena by placing them under arrest. "From that day onward," the chronicler reports, Ivan "forbade their names to be mentioned in prayers and litanies and forbade . . . [Dmitri] to be called Grand Prince." Three days later he bestowed the title of "Autocrat of All Russia" on Vasili, explaining merely that Dmitri had been rude to him. Elena's death in 1504 and Dmitri's in 1509 put an end to the scheming once and for all. Even their deaths seem to have been the result of foul play: in the sixteenth century it was widely believed that Dmitri had succumbed to either starvation or suffocation.

In 1505, Ivan the Great died and Vasili ascended the throne. He was in many ways a worthy successor. Like Ivan, he ruled autocratically, continuing the twin policies of political centralization and unification of the Great Russian territories. In 1510, for example, Vasili arbitrarily seized Pskov, and in order to secure his hold on the principality followed the precedent set by Ivan thirty-two years earlier in Novgorod: he forcibly re-

moved the city's most successful citizens and replaced them with loyal Muscovites. Thus deprived of their leaders, the Pskovians were unable to resist annexation.

A man of sophisticated tastes in art, Vasili III continued to sponsor the remodeling of the Kremlin. The Cathedral of the Archangel Michael was completed, as was the Terem Palace, which in 1508 became the residence of the grand prince and his consort Solomonia. Furthermore, Vasili commissioned artists to decorate many of the Kremlin churches. They covered the walls, pillars, and arches with Byzantine-style frescoes and finished the murals in the Uspenski sobor. When the grand prince entered the newly embellished cathedral in 1515 he was so overcome with emotion that he likened its atmosphere to heaven itself.

Indeed, by the early sixteenth century the Moscow citadel was an imposing capital whose beauty evoked much favorable comment. Yet Westerners still looked down upon Russia, doubting that it had fully cast off its barbaric heritage. These impressions were substantiated by the observations of such visitors as Baron Sigismund von Herberstein, who served as ambassador from the Holy Roman Empire to Moscow in 1517 and again in 1526.

In his fascinating account of the customs and style of life in Muscovy, Herberstein made some startling revelations. He reported that every Muscovite considered himself a serf of the prince, and that the "people enjoy slavery more than freedom." As soon as a person was freed from personal bondage to one master, he immediately sold himself to another. When suspected thieves were apprehended, "the order is, that they shall first have their heels broken, and then rest

Russia's first native saints, Vladimir of Kiev and his ill-fated sons Boris and Gleb, dominate the central panel of the complex biographical icon above. Surrounding vignettes depict the death of Vladimir and the assassination of his warrior-sons by their half brother. Frescoes depicting the full panoply of Russian saints cover the interior of the Cathedral of the Archangel Michael (opposite).

two or three days while they swell, and then . . . they make them walk again."

Herberstein also recorded the wretched manner in which Russian women were treated. They were rarely permitted to leave the house, even to attend church, and it was generally acknowledged that the female was inherently impure.

Grand Prince Vasili III himself is reputed to have treated his wife most cruelly, though his actions can be attributed to extenuating circumstances. During their many years of marriage, Solomonia had failed to bear any children. The grand prince lacked confidence in his brother's ability to rule effectively, and consequently the question of the succession obsessed him.

The barrenness of his wife tormented Vasili to such an extent that when he came upon a bird's nest during a trip to northern Russia he cried out: "I feel sadness. To whom could I liken myself? Not to the birds — they bear offspring; not to the animals — they are prolific; not to the streams — they play with waves and abound in fish." Looking at the ground, he continued his lament: "Oh Lord! And not to the earth can I liken myself, since it produces fruit and thus glorifies Thee!" In 1525 he put an end to his agony by divorcing Solomonia despite the Church's refusal to give its approval.

A few months later Vasili married Elena Glinskaia, a Lithuanian princess of German origin. In 1530 she bore him a son, baptized Ivan. Had Vasili not abandoned his first wife, Russia might have been spared a ghastly period in her history. For his son by Elena was to become one of the Kremlin's most notorious rulers, the infamous Ivan the Terrible.

III

Ivan the Awe-inspiring

A famous jester is said to have approached Tsar Ivan IV one day and offered him some fine raw meat. The tsar refused, angrily declaring that he never ate meat on fast days. "But how is that?" the jester retorted. "Why, you eat human flesh." The ruler who inspired this story has aroused intense curiosity and equally intense revulsion for more than four centuries. Mercurial, colorful, articulate, and thoroughly unscrupulous, Ivan has been the subject of numerous volumes. And because many documents relating to his reign have been destroyed by fire, his biographers have enjoyed ample opportunity for guesswork and fanciful interpretations.

Some historians have depicted Ivan as a demented sadist and lecher whose main goal in life was to satisfy his basest instincts and whose policies ultimately led to the collapse of the state. Others have praised him — without necessarily condoning his crimes — as a gifted leader who subjugated the selfish feudal lords and established a personal autocracy that not only unified the state but extended its power. One of the most respected representatives of this latter school, the Soviet historian Robert Wipper, flatly states that "the enhanced attention to Ivan's . . . cruelties, the stern and withering moral verdicts on his personality, the proneness to regard him as a man of unbalanced mind, all belong to the age of sentimental enlightenment and high society liberalism." Finally, several historians stress that despite Ivan's personal aberrations he was beloved by the people, who looked upon him as pious and well-intentioned. Indeed, it seems certain that in his own time he acquired the epithet *Grozny* — which is generally translated as "terrible" but can also mean

"awe-inspiring" — not because of his immoral conduct but because the common folk considered him their champion against the enemies of Muscovy.

The portrait of Ivan that emerges from the few surviving records of his reign is so nebulous that each of these appraisals contains an element of plausibility. In fact, his most enduring trait appears to have been his "moral instability." In his personal life and in affairs of state he regularly alternated between "lofty mental flights and shameful moral degradations." Thus he meticulously adhered to religious ritual, often rising at 4:00 A.M. to pray for two or three hours. Yet when it suited his purposes, he defied the Church and disregarded its teachings. In 1568, for example, he publicly humiliated a popular metropolitan who had dared to criticize his conduct; a year later the ecclesiastic was dead, either strangled or burned alive by one of the ruler's closest servants. Similarly, Ivan was genuinely devoted to his first wife, but within eleven days of her death he chose her successor. He also cherished his eldest son and carefully supervised his upbringing but in a fit of rage bludgeoned him so severely that the young man died.

The contradictory impulses that inhabited Ivan's soul were nowhere more apparent than in the political arena. On the positive side, he introduced imaginative reforms in several branches of government, cowed the unruly boyars, and scored a succession of stunning victories over the troublesome Tatars. Yet he governed with such recklessness and barbaric cruelty that when he departed the throne his politically unstable country was on the verge of economic ruin. On the mere suspicion that Novgorod was planning to betray him he had the city sacked and 60,000 men, women, and children massacred — but he took pains to send lists of victims to various monasteries so that requiem masses could be performed in their honor. He even made generous personal contributions to help defray the cost of those rituals.

Although a professed believer in the divine origin of autocratic power, Ivan in practice made a mockery of this principle of government. In 1575, for example, he whimsically conferred his crown upon an obscure Tatar prince, Simeon Bekbulatovich, and retired to Moscow to live as a humble boyar. Bekbulatovich made a pretense of governing, although he does not seem to have exercised any real power. In 1576 Ivan ended the grotesque joke and reascended the throne, to rule for another eight years. There was surely a touch of madness in all this, but if we assess the total impact of Ivan's policies on Russia, we are tempted to agree with the historian who described his system of rule as "the madness of a genius."

The tsar's lack of equilibrium can be accounted for quite easily. Given his childhood experiences, it would have been remarkable if he had grown up to be a well-balanced adult. The death of his father when Ivan was only three had plunged the Kremlin into a ferocious duel for power between rival factions. Initially Ivan's mother, Elena, had acted as regent, but she subsequently — and rather foolishly — allowed herself to be influenced by her lover, Prince Orchin-Telepnov-Obolensky, a dolt devoid of political wisdom. Sensing weakness at the core of the government, a number of princes and boyars began to plot the regent's ouster. Within a year the country seemed to be on the brink of

civil war, and Elena managed to survive the crisis only by seizing the most dangerous conspirators, among them her close relatives, and throwing them into dungeons. Her victory was short-lived, however, for in 1538 she suddenly and mysteriously died. Many people thought she had been poisoned.

His mother's death deeply wounded the young boy and further isolated him from those he loved. Only two adults remained close to Ivan, his nanny and Prince Obolensky, and the boyars soon removed them from the Kremlin in order to eliminate all possible opposition to their quest for power. Alone and only eight years old, Ivan was obliged to stand by as Muscovy's rival factions, the Shuiskys and the Belskys, jostled ruthlessly for position. For a few years power seesawed between the two families: whichever faction held sway massacred members of the opposition — on occasion in full view of the lad — and plundered the state treasury. The Shuiskys even had the audacity to melt down valuable vessels in the royal palace and recast them into gold and silver plates bearing the names of their ancestors. Nominally, Muscovy was ruled by an oligarchy, but disorder verging on anarchy spread throughout the land.

Neither faction paid much attention to young Ivan. From time to time he was allowed to don his regalia and participate in official ceremonies, but generally the ruling cliques ignored him and even deprived him of adequate clothing and food. The spiteful Shuiskys also decided to murder his one friend, a boyar named Fedor Vorontsov, because Vorontsov did not belong to their clique. They were about to flog him to death in one of the rooms of the palace when

Byzantine filigree work, mastered by Russian artisans in the late fifteenth century, gives Ivan IV's crown (left) a delicacy that contradicts the tsar's awesome reputation. Ivan's "Kazan Hat," studded with rubies, pearls, and turquoises — and capped by a single uncut topaz — commemorates the tsar's decisive victory over the Tatars in 1552. Eighteen years later, Novgorod fell victim to an equally savage attack by Ivan's troops. That incident, which is the subject of the historical icon at right, resulted in the decimation of the city (lower right) and the slaughter of some 60,000 of its defenseless citizens.

Ivan intervened; Vorontsov's life was spared, but he was exiled to Kostroma, a city northeast of Moscow.

The most frightening event of Ivan's minority occurred in 1542, when Ivan Shuisky led an army against Ivan Fedorovich Belsky, then in power. The metropolitan, who had sided with Belsky, sought refuge in the tsar's palace in the Kremlin, but this did not deter Shuisky, who ordered his troops to capture the dignitary at all costs. When they burst into the royal bedroom in the middle of the night, unceremoniously awakening the grand prince from deep slumber, the boy assumed that Shuisky's minions had come to assassinate him. It soon became apparent that they were only interested in carrying out their orders, however, and Ivan's timely intervention again prevented a murder. Instead, the metropolitan was deposed and banished to a monastery.

Ivan never forgot this incident, nor the other humiliations of his childhood. These experiences engendered in him a profound hostility toward the boyars — and, more significantly, a lasting distrust of people in general. Nor is it any wonder that the violence and bestiality he observed every day rendered him callous and even cruel. (Indeed, the Shuiskys deliberately fostered the lad's sadistic instincts so as to divert him from politics.) By the time Ivan was ten years old, a biographer reports, his "great amusement was to throw dogs down from the top of the castle terraces and enjoy their anguish." And when he was thirteen he "began to go about the streets . . . thrashing the men he met, violating the women, and always applauded by those about him."

The boyars who encouraged this behavior were too shortsighted to realize that someday Ivan might turn his rage against them — which he did as early as 1543, the year he first began to assert his authority. He ordered the arrest of Andrei Shuisky, then leader of his party, and when the soldiers took it upon themselves to strangle the prince, Ivan gave no sign of displeasure. During the next four years the grand prince, surrounded by a group of young, wealthy frolickers, indulged his every whim. At this early stage of his career Ivan also demonstrated that he could be a capricious sovereign: in 1546 he ordered his friend Vorontsov executed for treason, although the evidence against him was inconclusive.

But Ivan was not simply a playboy and sadist. Intelligent, well-read, and fiercely ambitious, he felt destined for a place in history through his role as the nation's leader. Accordingly, early in 1547 he took the unprecedented step of having himself formally crowned in the Uspenski sobor as Tsar and Autocrat of All the Russias. During the ceremony the claim was put forth that the cross and regalia on Ivan's head and shoulders had been sent to the Grand Prince of Kiev in the twelfth century by the Byzantine Emperor Constantin Monomachus. To lend weight to this suggestion that he was the successor of the Eastern emperors, Ivan then followed Byzantine tradition in choosing a bride. He directed all the nobles in his realm — those who refused faced execution — to send their marriageable daughters to Moscow. About 1,500 maidens were gathered in a huge building where they slept twelve to a room. Together with an adviser, Ivan inspected the entire seraglio and "presented each fair lady with a kerchief embroidered with gold and gems, which he threw upon

her bosom." His choice made, "gifts were bestowed on the companions of the bride, and they were sent back to their own homes."

Ivan's choice was Anastasia Romanovna, who belonged to the nonprincely family of Zakharin-Iuriev. The tsar's decision dismayed Muscovite high society. "The sovereign offended us," Prince Semen Lobanov-Rostovsky complained, "by his marriage, taking a boyar's daughter, his slave, for bride. And we have to serve her as if she were our sister." But Ivan had chosen wisely. Warm, gentle, affectionate, and loyal, Anastasia was one of the few people with whom the tsar felt at ease, and she was one of the few he fully trusted.

Shortly after his marriage, Ivan faced a series of crises that sorely tested his skills as ruler. In his handling of them we can observe how he gradually changed from a cynical despot into a shrewd politician. In June 1547, several citizens of Pskov visited the tsar in the village of Ostrovka to complain about the arbitrary actions of their governor. Ivan responded to their petition by having boiling brandy poured on them and having their hair and beards singed by candles. The unfortunate delegation had just undressed and lain down on the floor, preparatory to execution, when an excited messenger interrupted the proceedings with dreadful news. A new fire — one of a series that had erupted in Moscow in recent months — was raging in the capital, and the whole city was threatened with destruction. The tsar abruptly halted the torture and turned his attention to the catastrophe.

The devastation in the capital proved staggering. Twenty-five thousand houses were destroyed, and at least 17,000 Muscovites were burned to death. Over 80,000 people were left homeless, including many nobles who lived inside the Kremlin walls. The tsar's own palace, the metropolitan's palace, the treasury building, the arsenal, two monasteries, and several churches — all within the citadel — had been reduced to ashes, and the cupola of Fieraventi's famous Cathedral of the Assumption had been consumed by flames. For a time Ivan was obliged to forsake the Kremlin for the nearby village of Vorobievo.

The dazed survivors could not believe that a disaster of such magnitude was accidental, and they began to look for scapegoats. Before long the story gained currency that sorcerers had torn human hearts out of corpses, dipped them into pails of water, and then spread the fire by sprinkling the streets with this brew. When some boyars attested to having observed this very practice, suspects were promptly arrested, tortured to yield confessions, and executed.

But the aroused Muscovites were not satisfied. Many interpreted the fire as divine punishment for Ivan's sins, and they openly advocated rebellion. At the same time a group of boyars circulated the rumor that the Glinskys, a powerful family at court, had caused the conflagration. These boyars summoned the populace to a general meeting in front of the Uspenski sobor, where one of them demanded to know who had burned the city. "Princess Anna Glinskaia [Ivan's maternal grandmother] through sorcery," roared the crowd — whereupon the boyars urged the people to seek revenge on the Glinskys. Prince Iuri Glinsky, Ivan's uncle, had overheard the outburst and taken refuge in the Uspenski sobor. The enraged plebeians, in no mood to respect the sanctity of the church, dragged the prince from his

The disastrous flash fire that swept the Russian capital in 1547 left 80,000 Muscovites homeless, among them Ivan and his wife, Anastasia (left), who fled the conflagration in a covered sleigh. Another miniature by the contemporary chronicler Nikonov Letopis records the fervor with which Ivan restored both the citadel and the capital once the flames subsided. Within two years, all the fire damage had been repaired and a new royal residence had been added to the Kremlin compound (right).

hiding place, assassinated him, and exhibited his corpse in the marketplace — a practice generally reserved for convicted criminals. For the next two days the crowd roamed the streets of Moscow in search of members of the Glinsky family.

Not finding Iuri's mother in Moscow, the mob assumed that she had sought the tsar's protection and marched on to Vorobievo. The commoners refused to believe Ivan when he disavowed knowledge of Anna Glinskaia's whereabouts, and they actually threatened to kill him if he did not cooperate. After some heated exchanges he managed to persuade them that he was speaking the truth, and many began to have second thoughts about their conduct. Shrewdly taking advantage of the crowd's vacillation, Ivan quickly ordered the seizure and execution of the ringleaders. This resolute action enabled the tsar to weather the crisis, but the events had taken their toll: Ivan came close to having a nervous breakdown.

When Ivan regained his equilibrium, he seemed more mature, responsible, and wise than ever before. He recruited thoughtful counselors and introduced policies that augured well for Muscovy. He publicized these policies, as well as the principles that would guide him as sovereign, at a mass meeting in Red (or Beautiful) Square, a large oblong plaza just outside the Kremlin walls. Since the early sixteenth century Red Square had served as the city's marketplace; earlier it had been the scene of several battles with the Tatars. There Muscovites gathered to hear official announcements and the latest gossip or to witness the torture of prisoners.

Two years after the fire, in 1549, Ivan treated the people assembled in Red Square to an altogether unusual spectacle, a public confession by the ruler himself. After denouncing the boyars for exploiting his subjects, he acknowledged his past failure to protect them from "oppression and extortion." Then, identifying himself fully with the common folk, he called for a new era of Christian love. "Henceforth," he vowed, "I will be your judge and defender." This speech, both brilliant and demagogic, did much to raise his popularity among the people.

During the next few years Ivan's constructive domestic program and military successes contributed to a constant increase in his stature. He strove to eliminate corruption among government officials, introduced a measure of local self-government, modernized the army, improved judicial procedures, and attempted to root out abuses in the Church. The image of himself that he wished to convey is expressed most graphically in his Kremlin palace — known as the Middle Golden because of its gilded roof — whose inner walls were adorned with frescoes depicting an entire conception of government. Although inspired by the priest Sylvester, one of Ivan's advisers, their content is largely secular: the tsar appears as a righteous judge, courageous warrior, disburser of alms to the poor, and sovereign crushing the enemies of the state. In one mural he is shown in the act of pouring water to sanctify the people.

The major reason for Ivan's popularity at midcentury was his decisive blow against the Tatars, whose murderous raids into Muscovite territory had not ceased altogether. In addition to plundering Russian cities, the Tatars made a practice of capturing Russians

and selling them as slaves. It has been estimated that in 1551 some 100,000 Muscovites languished in prisons in Kazan, the Tatar khanate closest to Moscow. That year Ivan personally led an army of 150,000 men against Kazan, and in 1552, after a series of bloody clashes, he succeeded in capturing the city.

Ivan's victory was greeted with jubilation, and throngs of people lined a four-mile stretch of the Iauza River to catch a glimpse of the returning warrior. Joyously, the commoners kissed his feet, hands, and clothes and proclaimed him "Conqueror of the Barbarians — Defender of the Christians." In the words of one biographer, their delight "was so mingled with religious fervor that they showed towards him something of the adoration that they might have shown the Savior himself." Four years later Ivan neutralized another Tatar stronghold by capturing Astrakhan. Muscovy then controlled the entire basin of the Volga, and thereafter Russians could colonize lands in the south, southwest, and east. The path to Siberia had been opened at last.

Even before the annexation of Astrakhan, Ivan decided to erect a new church in honor of his victories. Between 1553 and 1560 the somewhat bizarre Cathedral of Saint Basil the Blessed was built at the southern end of Red Square. Ivan was so proud of the new building he allegedly ordered that the Italian architect who designed it be blinded — so that he might never surpass this masterpiece. Although the story has been told many times, it is known to be apocryphal. In truth, the cathedral was designed by two Russian architects, Postnik and Barma, and it is generally thought to typify medieval Russian architecture.

Based on the wooden churches then prevalent in villages around Moscow, Saint Basil's is quite unlike the cathedrals inside the Kremlin. The structure consists of a central stone church surrounded by nine smaller churches, each commemorating one of Muscovy's military triumphs over the Tatars. Each of the churches is linked to its neighbors by passages, and each is roofed with a bulbous cupola. Because of its diversity of ornamental detail, its apparent lack of symmetry, and, in time, its coloring — red, orange, yellow, green, blue, violet, gold, and silver — the Cathedral of Saint Basil the Blessed was for a long time the object of ridicule. But today the consensus is that the various elements add up to a harmonious and stunning architectural whole.

Despite his domestic and military achievements, Ivan remained too suspicious of his boyars to enjoy peace of mind. By the mid-1550's his position on the throne was secure, but he could never free himself from the fear that at the first sign of weakness the nobles would betray him. Although the fears were probably exaggerated, the boyars' behavior during one crisis certainly gave him fresh cause to doubt that they had learned much since the chaotic days of the late 1530's and the early 1540's.

In 1553 Ivan suddenly developed a high fever. His doctors could find no cure and gave up hope of saving his life. On his deathbed Ivan proclaimed his son Dmitri, an infant, as his successor, and he called upon the boyars to swear an oath of allegiance to his heir. Several dignitaries demurred on the grounds that they feared another period of anarchy if the infant ascended the throne. The real reason for their recalcitrance was less noble: they simply did not wish to take orders from

The Cathedral of Saint Basil the Blessed, which dominates the southern end of Red Square (above), is unquestionably the most arresting structure in Moscow. Its bulbous, polychrome cupolas, florid scrollwork, and riotously eclectic brickwork (left) give Saint Basil the Blessed an aura of whimsicality that contrasts sharply with the dour austerity of the nearby Kremlin. Although persistent legend attributes the design of Saint Basil to an Italian, the cathedral was actually built by two native architects named Barmen and Posnik Iakolav. Its appearance is unmistakably Russian, reflecting the motifs common to the famed wooden churches of northern Russia. Like the most famous of those older structures, the Church of the Transfiguration at Kizha, Saint Basil's is actually a cluster of buildings — a central church surrounded by nine auxiliary churches, eight dedicated to Ivan IV's eight victories over the Tatars and a ninth consecrated to Moscow's holy beggar, Saint Basil. Its whitewashed exterior was painted in its present rainbow hues (right) in the seventeenth century — a departure that prompted the Marquis de Custine, a saturnine and openly critical visitor to Moscow, to liken Saint Basil's to a box of glazed fruit. Another critic labeled the church "the dream of a diseased imagination." These contemptuous foreigners failed to realize what modern art critics readily acknowledge — namely that Saint Basil's combines the vibrant palette, bold patterns, and unrestrained exuberance that are the quintessence of Russian folk art.

the lowly Zakharini, the relatives of Ivan's wife who would have ruled during Dmitri's minority. More important, the boyars themselves wanted to seize power. While Ivan lay on his bed in agonizing pain, he could hear the boyars quarreling about the succession in an adjoining room. The tsar could not help suspecting that as soon as he died the contentious boyars would slaughter his entire family. He ultimately prevailed upon most of them to sign the oath, but he put little trust in their word.

Miraculously, Ivan recovered from the illness — only to suffer an overwhelming personal loss. In order to offer thanks to the Lord for restoring his health, he undertook a long and arduous pilgrimage to the Kirillo-Belozersky monastery with his wife and infant son — and while the royal party was changing boats on the Shesna River, a nurse accidentally dropped the baby into the water. The child drowned, and the tsar returned to the Kremlin an embittered man.

For several years Ivan kept his inner rage under control. Then several events occurred to completely unsettle him. First, his beloved Anastasia died in 1560 — a loss whose importance it is hard to exaggerate, for she had exercised a soothing influence on the tsar that curbed his most violent instincts. Shortly thereafter he dismissed two of his most sensible advisers, Sylvester and Adashev. Both had for some reason been hostile toward Anastasia, and Ivan had convinced himself that the two had caused her death by deliberately failing to obtain the necessary medical supplies. Four years later Prince Andrei Kurbsky, one of Ivan's most distinguished generals, defected to Lithuania, apparently out of fear that the tsar would also turn against him. News

of the defection infuriated Ivan and reinforced his lack of trust in the boyars. After brooding over these events for several months, he inaugurated a series of policies that are among the most outlandish both in Russian and in world history.

One day late in 1564 Ivan and his family quietly departed from the Kremlin. Their destination was the village of Alexandrovsk, to which the tsar's personal effects as well as his sacred images, crosses, and treasure chests had already been sent. In the meantime two royal proclamations were issued in Moscow. The first reminded the citizenry of the brutal conduct of the boyars during Ivan's childhood, disparaged their loyalty to tsar and Church, and announced the sovereign's sorrowful decision to abdicate. The second, addressed to the commoners of the realm, suggested that Ivan did not really expect his abdication to be taken seriously. Its assurances of concern for the people's welfare were clearly designed to provoke so strong an outcry over the tsar's departure that he would be able to return to power with greater authority than ever.

Ivan had judged the people's mood with uncanny shrewdness. As one historian has noted: "Everyone stood petrified at the proceedings. Shops were closed, offices deserted, and voices hushed. Then, in a panic of terror, the city broke forth into lamentations, and besought the metropolitan, the bishops, and certain of the boyars to go to Alexandrovsk, and to beg the tsar not to abandon his realm."

When the emissaries from Moscow arrived in Alexandrovsk, Ivan had a prepared statement in readiness. He agreed to reassume the burdens of office, but only if the populace would accept certain conditions that

he intended to elaborate at a later date. The emissaries felt they could not reject this novel arrangement and retired to Moscow to await the tsar's pleasure. When Ivan returned to the Kremlin in February 1565, his appearance had been totally transformed. Whether from genuine torment over the advisability of resuming power or from anxiety that his stratagem might boomerang, the thirty-five-year-old tsar had become an old man in the short period of eight weeks: "His small, gray, piercing eyes had grown dull, his hitherto animated, kindly face had fallen in and now bore a misanthropic expression, and only a few stray remnants remained of his once abundant hair and beard." The change, it soon turned out, was more than physical. Ivan had decided on an entirely new regime, under which all traitors would summarily be executed and all boyars he deemed disloyal would be banished from court. In effect, the new order amounted to nothing less than a monstrous police dictatorship.

To help root out sedition, he established the so-called *oprichnina,* a separate state with its own administration directly under his authority. Thousands of people were evicted from their homes and replaced with loyal supporters, a process of expropriation that continued until the *oprichnina* encompassed almost one half of the state. In addition, Ivan created a special police force, the "Blackness of Hell," whose members dressed in black clothes, rode black horses, and carried a dog's head and a broom. Their duty was to sweep treason from the land and eliminate the tsar's enemies.

Shortly thereafter Ivan moved back to Alexandrovsk, where, in order to establish a haven from intrigue and treason, he converted his lodgings into a fortified monastery. There he surrounded himself with three hundred specially selected *oprichniki* who formed a "brotherhood" of which he was the "abbot." At four o'clock in the morning, every member of the brotherhood was expected to appear in the chapel for two hours of prayer; anyone who missed one of these devotional sessions faced imprisonment for eight days. In keeping with the duality of the tsar's nature, the members of the brotherhood also treated their worldly appetites to sumptuous dinners, unspeakable orgies, and frequent visits to the torture chambers.

In the rest of the country Ivan now unleashed a reign of terror. Many innocent people were slaughtered on the slightest pretext — and often on no pretext at all. In a contemporary account, Heinrich von Staden, a German adventurer who served in the *oprichnina,* describes how Ivan impulsively murdered one of Muscovy's leading boyars, Ivan Petrovich Cheliadin, and threw the corpse into a filthy pit. "The grand prince," von Staden continues, "then went with his *oprichniki* and burned all the [landed estates] . . . in the country belonging to this Ivan Petrovich. The villages were burned with their churches and everything that was in them, icons and church ornaments. Women and girls were stripped naked and forced in that state to catch chickens in the fields." Most of the time the *oprichniki* did not content themselves with subjecting women to such harmless indignities; a favorite sport was rape, and Tsar Ivan not only approved but participated in it.

After a few years Ivan turned against the leading *oprichniki,* probably because he believed that they, too, had committed treason. He justified the action by

In a determined effort to establish diplomatic contact with the West, Ivan ordered that a Foreign Office be constructed inside the Kremlin walls in 1565. When it was finished, he dispatched a number of official delegations to Western Europe. The contingent that reached Emperor Maximilian II's court in 1576 is pictured in this contemporary engraving. Led by a sumptuously robed ambassador, colorfully dressed boyars arrive bearing dozens of animal pelts, Russia's most prized export.

spuriously claiming that they had disregarded his orders in committing atrocities. The slaughter of the *oprichniki* was accomplished in the style to which they were accustomed. Thus, according to von Staden, one prince was "chopped to death by the harquebusiers with axes or halberds. Prince Vasili Temkin was drowned. . . . Peter Seisse was hanged from his own court gate opposite the bedroom. Prince Andrei Ovtsyn was hanged in the Arbatskaya Street of the *oprichnina*. A living sheep was hung next to him. Marshal Bulat . . . was killed and his sister raped by five hundred harquebusiers. The captain of the harquebusiers, Kuraka Unkovskii, was killed and stuck under the ice." Ivan even ordered that the handsome young Fedor Basmanov, with whom the tsar had indulged in homosexual relations, be brutally put to death. Before being executed, these dignitaries were publicly whipped in the marketplace and forced to sign over all their money and land to the crown.

It is not known exactly how many people perished during the *oprichnina's* seven-year existence, but the number surely ran into the thousands. Insofar as the terror was designed to weaken the powerful aristocrats and eradicate separatist sentiments, it no doubt succeeded — and in so doing laid the basis for the subsequent development of untrammeled autocracy in Russia. Furthermore, Ivan emerged from the carnage as a ruler whose authority no one dared challenge.

The *oprichnina's* reign of terror so weakened the country militarily that in 1571 Ivan could not fend off a Tatar army that plundered a large portion of the capital. He was also too weak to realize one of his most cherished dreams, the annexation of Livonia, which would have given Muscovy control over the Baltic. Time and again he attempted to conquer the territory, but in the end he had to acknowledge failure.

Personal happiness eluded Ivan during these years of turmoil. He had never loved his second wife, Maria — who allegedly possessed morals "as loose as her instincts were fierce" — and soon after her death in 1569 he sought a third. From the two thousand virgins brought to Moscow for his inspection, Ivan personally selected twelve finalists. Then he bade his private doctor and some old women at court to settle on the most beautiful, intelligent, and upright — warning them in advance that he would not tolerate snoring. The choice fell on Marfa Sobakin, the attractive daughter of a Novgorod merchant, but she became mortally ill the moment she learned of the tsar's decision. The wedding ceremony took place nevertheless, but even before the marriage was consummated the bride passed away. Loath to admit the reason for her death, Ivan claimed that Marfa had been poisoned — a contention he then advanced in support of his petition to the Church for permission to marry a fourth time. His fourth union ended after three years, however, when he sent his wife to a monastery on charges of having plotted treason. Thereafter, he married at least three more times, always without ecclesiastical sanction.

While living with his third common-law wife, Ivan hatched one of his more preposterous schemes. He took it into his head to marry Lady Mary Hastings, an Englishwoman of royal blood, and in 1581 he dispatched Fedor Pisemski to London to look her over. Ivan specifically requested that he note "her complexion, her figure, her proportions," and obtain her portrait.

Queen Elizabeth I was horrified by the idea, but because she craved privileges for her traders in Muscovy — who had been active since 1553 — she did not refuse outright. She managed to delay giving an audience to Pisemski for some time — and when she did, she assured him that the tsar, favoring beautiful women as he did, would not care for the homely Lady Hastings, who was just recovering from smallpox and looked especially unappealing at that moment.

After several months of petty delays and frustrated negotiations, the Muscovite ambassador was at last allowed to see the elusive Lady Hastings. It soon became evident that she had no interest in moving to Moscow, but Ivan would not give up. He continued to press for an Anglo-Saxon bride, but before a willing candidate was found, he died.

It is doubtful whether Ivan could have sustained a harmonious relationship with any woman during his last few years, much less with a stranger from the West. For after November 1581, when he unintentionally killed his son and heir, Ivan, the tsar passed most of his days in a state of near-hysteria. According to the most plausible account, the tragic incident was triggered by an earlier encounter between the tsar and his daughter-in-law, who was then pregnant. Ivan came upon her clad only in a nightgown and was shocked by her immodesty. Losing his self-control, he slapped the woman so hard that within a day she miscarried. When the tsarevich complained to his father, Ivan again lost his temper and violently struck his son with the iron-tipped staff that he always carried with him. Unhappily, the blow fell on the tsarevich's temple and knocked him to the ground, where he bled profusely. Despite

the heroic efforts of the court doctors and the sovereign's fervent prayers, the twenty-seven-year-old heir to the throne died four days later.

The tsar was overcome with grief and self-pity. Unable to sleep at night, he would wander aimlessly through the palace, weeping and bellowing in despair, finally collapsing from exhaustion. After remaining prostrate for a while he would resume his wandering and wailing. Convinced that his son's death was God's punishment for his sins, Ivan called his boyars together and, pronouncing himself unworthy to rule, asked them to choose a successor. Suspecting a trap — and convinced that Ivan was merely testing their loyalty — the boyars pleaded with him to stay in power. The grief-stricken tsar obliged, although he was by this time a broken man, much of the time incapable of exercising effective leadership.

In the spring of 1584 Ivan became seriously ill for the last time. Characteristically, he conformed to his lifelong patterns of behavior even on his deathbed. On the one hand, the tsar urged his advisers and especially his remaining heir, Fedor, to avoid war with Christian princes, reduce taxes, and rule justly. On the other, he continued to indulge his appetite for physical excesses. In one of the basest acts of his career, he made "an abominable attempt" on Fedor's wife, Irina, whom he had previously treated as a daughter. Then, when his illness had run its course and he knew himself to be near death, he took monastic vows — in the expectation, no doubt, that he could thus atone for his innumerable sins. He died as he had lived, a man who oscillated between acts of gross depravity and occasional demonstrations of virtue.

IV
Troubled Times

The death of Ivan IV in 1584 left Muscovy in the incompetent hands of his twenty-seven-year-old son, Fedor. During his childhood Fedor had been an "undersized, white-faced stripling who was disposed to dropsy and possessed of an unsteady, quasi-senile gait." He grew into a feebleminded adult far more interested in spiritual matters than affairs of state. When he received foreign dignitaries, he could not refrain from "smiling, nor from gazing first upon his scepter, and then upon his orb." Nothing gave him greater pleasure than to run from one church to another ringing the bells and having mass celebrated. As Ivan himself sadly noted, Fedor behaved more like a sexton than the son of a tsar.

Under the best of circumstances, it would have been foolhardy to entrust the helm of state to a man so lacking in ability — and these were not the best of circumstances. Fedor's accession portended disaster, for by the 1580's Russia was rife with discontent, mainly as a result of Ivan's recent military failures and harsh domestic program. An English visitor accurately described the mood of the nation in 1588–89: Ivan's "wicked policy and tyrannous practice (though now it be ceased) hath so troubled the country and filled it so full of grudge and mortal hatred ever since, that it will not be quenched (as it seemeth now) till it burn again into a civil flame." Although a series of palace intrigues did occur, catastrophe was averted for two decades, chiefly as a result of the astute and sensible policies of the man who ultimately emerged as the power behind the Russian throne.

The struggle for influence over the imbecile tsar began fifteen days after his father's death. On April 2, 1584, Prince Bogdan Belsky, one of Ivan's favorites, lingered unobtrusively inside the Kremlin until the other boyars had departed for dinner. With the help of *streltsy* — specially trained and privileged musketeers — he stealthily closed the gates to the citadel. He then met alone with Fedor and implored the sovereign to reestablish the *oprichnina* with Belsky himself as its head. In this way the prince expected to undermine the other notables, most of whom recoiled at the idea of reverting to Ivan's terror.

Word somehow reached the boyars that Belsky was alone with the tsar. Suspecting the prince's intentions, they rushed to the Kremlin, only to find armed *streltsy* blocking the gates. After indignant protests and prolonged discussion two nobles were allowed to enter. Fearing for their comrades' lives, the remaining boyars set to screaming so loudly that the *streltsy* thrashed several of the offenders. The din attracted a large crowd, among whom the story rapidly circulated that Belsky was on the point of — or had already succeeded in — murdering the two boyar emissaries. The crowd, transformed by these rumors into a mob, burst into the Kremlin. The *streltsy* responded by opening fire, and within minutes twenty of the intruders lay dead on the pavement.

The mob was eventually beaten back, but the accompanying violence and bloodshed only further enraged the boyars, who made feverish plans to storm the fortress anew. In the meantime a few of their number managed to sneak through one of the gates to "liberate" the tsar. At this juncture both Fedor and his would-be adviser appeared before the throng and asked the reason for the commotion. The angry mob charged that Belsky intended to massacre the boyars and demanded that he be handed over to them. Fedor rejected this request but promised to exile the prince to Nizhni Novgorod.

A brief period of civil harmony followed, during which the aged boyar Nikita Iurev took over as the tsar's principal counselor. Upon Iurev's death in 1585 Prince Ivan Mstislavsky and a thirty-four-year-old boyar named Boris Godunov became the leading contenders for his position. In this struggle, Godunov enjoyed a number of advantages over his chief rival. Although barely literate, he had earned the favor of Ivan the Terrible by dint of his intelligence and good sense. Moreover, his marriage to the daughter of Malyuta Skuratov, a close friend of Ivan's and a notorious *oprichnik,* had brought him into the ruler's inner circle. Yet Godunov was in no way implicated in Ivan's excesses and had therefore not aroused the enmity of the boyars whom the tsar had persecuted. Boris had been present during a lamentable contretemps between Ivan and his son and had intervened when the tsar was about to strike the heir-apparent, an action that earned him a blow to his body. Later a grateful Ivan showered affection on the boyar.

But Boris's major source of influence emanated from his sister Irina, who was Tsar Fedor's wife. Indeed, so firmly entrenched was he at the imbecile's court that he quickly overpowered his rival for the sovereign's favor. Under Ivan these intrigues had invariably ended with the spilling of blood, but Boris was content simply to exile Mstislavsky and a few of his supporters. He even allowed Mstislavsky's son to remain in Moscow and hold an important post.

It is interesting to note that Moussorgsky's opera *Boris Godunov,* based on a play by Pushkin, grossly distorts the character of Boris. Both these important works of art depict Godunov as corrupted by a lust for power. Neither Pushkin nor Moussorgsky seems to have been impressed by Godunov's lack of involvement in the earliest intrigues surrounding Fedor or by the boyar's benign treatment of his rival.

Boris's contemporaries were equally unimpressed by the boyar's fair-minded demeanor, and shortly after his triumph over Mstislavsky several Muscovite dignitaries attempted to oust him from power. The most fantastic plot against Boris was the one devised in 1587 by the princes Andrei and Ivan Shuisky in concert with the Metropolitan Dionysius. They organized a raucous demonstration in Red Square in support of their demand that Fedor divorce Irina, a demand based upon the allegation that the tsarina was barren. The intriguers, who knew that their accusation was untrue — the tsarina had in fact miscarried several times — obviously hoped that by getting rid of Irina they would remove the basis for Boris's influence at court. But they failed to reckon with the tsar's feelings for his wife. Fedor loved Irina and had not the slightest intention of abandoning her; instead he forced the metropolitan to resign, banished the Shuiskys from Moscow, and ordered the execution of six of the demonstrators.

Godunov was now the most powerful man at court. As such he administered the country virtually unopposed for the next ten years. He was granted the right to conduct correspondence with foreign governments, and he always received envoys from abroad immediately after they had been greeted by the tsar. The festivities in Boris's palace on these occasions were every bit as elaborate and lavish as those in Fedor's. Godunov did not lack for funds, thanks to the tsar's generosity. One contemporary estimated that the boyar's annual income exceeded 90,000 rubles, and English visitors to Moscow considered Boris so powerful that they referred to him as "lieutenant of the empire" and "lord protector of Russia."

Boris's rule proved to be enlightened as well as successful. He generally eschewed risky foreign adventures, made serious efforts to help the destitute, and tried to lighten the burden borne by the peasants. Through a series of shrewd if not altogether honorable maneuvers he succeeded in elevating the Moscow metropolitanate to a patriarchate. This change added substantially to the prestige of the Muscovite church — and also to that of the tsar and Godunov himself. Above all, the years from 1588 to 1598 were a period of internal calm, a welcome change after the tumult of Ivan's reign.

In 1598 Fedor died without leaving a single relative who could advance a legitimate claim to the throne — his only child, a daughter, had died four years earlier. On his deathbed he bestowed "the scepter of the tsardom" on his consort, but she declined to serve, preferring to enter a convent. The metropolitan therefore summoned a *zemski sobor,* or national assembly, to elect a tsar. Boris was naturally the leading candidate, but to everyone's surprise he stubbornly turned down every suggestion that he campaign for the position. Instead he retired to a monastery and announced that he would refuse the crown if it were offered to him. The crafty boyar actually longed to be tsar of Muscovy, but he did not want to be beholden to the *zemski sobor*

for his election, nor did he want the election to serve as a precedent.

If he was to be tsar, he intended to found a new dynasty, thus permitting his children to succeed him automatically. He probably counted on the inability of the assembly to agree on another candidate, a deadlock that would force the delegates to turn to him in the end. When precisely this did happen, the assembly held a special meeting in the Cathedral of the Assumption and, in effect, acceded to all of Godunov's stipulations. Even then the *zemski sobor* felt that it was necessary to organize a mass procession of Muscovites to proclaim loudly the people's support of Boris's election. It has been suggested by one commentator that the police actually staged the demonstration, compelling the people to appear in the streets "with copious tears and lamentations — so much so that a large number of persons who did not happen at the moment to have any tears ready were forced to daub their eyes with their spittle, in order to avert the batons of the police."

As ruler in his own right, Boris did not fare as well as he had previously. To be sure, he continued many of his enlightened policies, policies which in some respects anticipated the innovative work of Peter the Great. He recognized the need for Russians to master Western technology and technical skills, for example, and he therefore attempted to found a university in Moscow. But the clergy, who feared the introduction of heretical ideas from non-Orthodox countries, blocked the plan. Instead, Godunov sent eighteen young men to the West to study — a bold move that unfortunately had no impact on Russia, for not one of the eighteen returned.

In later centuries, Boris Godunov's name was to become synonymous with scheming regicide. In truth, the villain of Moussorgsky's opera Boris Godunov *was a competent and progressive ruler — qualities conveyed by the portrait above.*

Boris also encouraged various building projects throughout the country. While he was still acting as Fedor's chief administrator, he had a whitewashed brick wall erected around Moscow, and in 1597 he ordered a stone wall erected around Smolensk. In addition numerous fortresses, churches, governmental offices, and storehouses were built throughout the state. Probably the single most notable artistic achievement inspired by Godunov was the Belfry of Ivan Veliki (Ivan the Great), which stands between the cathedrals of the Assumption and the Archangel Michael. Built in 1600, the tower rises to 270 feet and remains to this day a commanding structure in the Kremlin.

In many respects, Boris Godunov turned out to be an unlucky sovereign. In the fall of 1601, for example, large areas of Russia were blanketed by a very early frost that destroyed much of the crop. Many people went hungry, and in order to provide work for the needy Godunov introduced the equivalent of a public works program: the building of a conduit for water from the Moscow River to the Kremlin. This measure only worsened the situation in the capital, however, for as soon as people in the country heard of the relief project they streamed into the city. The weather did not improve during the following two years, and food shortages became even more acute. Between 1601 and 1603, 100,000 people are believed to have died of starvation in Moscow; several hundred thousand more perished elsewhere in the country.

Not surprisingly, Godunov's reputation declined sharply during this period. The people held him responsible for their sufferings and readily believed the horrendous stories that the boyars hastened to circulate about him. They charged him with ruthless ambition, corruption, and such misdeeds as having Moscow raided in order to divert attention from domestic difficulties. He was even accused of poisoning Tsar Fedor. But the most startling charge of all — subsequently echoed by Pushkin and Moussorgsky — was that he had engineered the murder of Ivan the Terrible's last child, the nine-year-old Dmitri, in order to pave the way for his own accession to the throne. The events surrounding the death of Dmitri in 1591 are actually so bizarre and the accounts of them so contradictory that they may justly be considered one of Russia's most intriguing detective stories.

Dmitri was born in 1582 to Ivan's seventh wife, Maria Nagaia, but since the church normally permitted a man no more than three marriages (an exception had been made to allow Ivan to take a fourth wife), the youngster was canonically ineligible for the crown. Dmitri's mother harbored great ambitions for her son, however, and she would not relinquish his claim to what she considered his patrimony. In order to prevent Maria from plotting against Tsar Fedor, she and her entire family were exiled to Uglich, a town that Ivan had bequeathed to Dmitri as an appanage. There Maria and her relatives plied the boy with hatred for Fedor and Godunov — so much so that Dmitri used to direct his playmates to make snow statues of the despised leaders, whose heads, arms, and legs he would then chop off. "This," he declared, "I'll do to them when I become tsar." Godunov no doubt heard of these games through his informers, just as he heard of the frequent visits Maria paid to soothsayers to find out how long Tsar Fedor and the tsarina would live. He

probably also learned that by 1590 Maria had organized an elaborate conspiracy designed to wrest power for her son.

A few months later, in 1591, Dmitri suddenly died from mysterious knife wounds. The Nagois lost no time in charging that government agents had murdered the boy, and once this story spread, the people of Uglich staged a violent rebellion against the tsar's officials. At the same time, fires set by arsonists in the employ of the Nagois broke out in Moscow. The plan was to discredit the government and foment a national uprising, but Tsar Fedor's troops quelled the disorders within a few days. Maria was forced to take the veil, and many members of her family were exiled to remote provincial towns.

Godunov then appointed a commission to investigate the death of Dmitri, which it eventually determined to have been accidental. The boy had been playing a game known as *tychka,* in which the participant throws a knife that he holds by the blade so that it turns several times in flight before striking its target. While thus holding the knife, Dmitri had an epileptic seizure — he was known to be an epileptic — and in falling over, fatally stabbed himself. The explanation seems far-fetched, but the evidence leaves little doubt that this is precisely how the boy died. Nevertheless, when the story was revived — some twelve years after the accident — that Godunov had contrived the murder of Dmitri, many people accepted it.

In the face of these slanders and intrigues, Boris lost his composure and instituted a terroristic regime bound to horrify everyone who recalled the barbarities of Ivan the Terrible. People were encouraged to spy

Among the more preposterous accusations leveled at Godunov by his detractors was the charge that he had ordered his men to assassinate Ivan IV's surviving son, Dmitri, in 1591 (left). The circumstances surrounding the nine-year-old epileptic's death were indeed bizarre, but Godunov was plainly innocent of any wrongdoing. Cleared of the charges against him, he retaliated by instituting a virtual police state. As popular unrest grew, dissidents rallied behind two false Dmitris. The first (near right) posed a threat to Godunov in his last years; the second (far right) set up a rival administration to challenge Godunov's successor.

on each other and to report anyone who uttered a critical word about the sovereign. Slaves played an especially important role in this campaign of espionage, for the police paid them handsomely to inform on their masters. The police also employed felons to eavesdrop on nobles in the streets in order to discover plots against the ruler. The upshot was that "members of one and the same family feared to hold communication with their fellows; and even to pronounce the tsar's name became a misdemeanor for which a detective could seize the delinquent and hale him to prison." Those who were denounced often suffered disgrace, torture, and exile, and a few were executed. Godunov's new system of rule, although harsh, was still a far cry from the brutality of Ivan the Terrible. Many of Boris's victims survived the ordeal and later served in high government posts.

Although the growing opposition weakened Godunov politically, in itself it could not dislodge him from power. The intriguers therefore dreamed up another scheme, one surpassing in absurdity the charge that the tsar had ordered the murder of Dmitri. In a sudden reversal, they claimed that the assassination attempt had failed and that Dmitri, the "legitimate claimant" to the throne, was alive and eager to assume his rightful position. In 1604 a pretender known as the False Dmitri appeared in Poland and was received in semiprivate audience by King Sigismund, who recognized the potential usefulness of the imposter in subduing Muscovy. The pope and the Jesuits also supported the pretender — who had converted to Catholicism — in the hope that he would deliver the Muscovites over to the Roman Church.

In October 1604, the pretender led a motley army of three thousand Poles, Ukrainians, and Don Cossacks into Muscovy. The army met with little success until April 1605, when Boris died, probably as a result of poisoning. His son Fedor succeeded to the throne, only to be deposed a few weeks later. Both boyars and commoners went over to the False Dmitri in large numbers, and in June 1605 the imposter triumphantly entered the Kremlin and butchered the Godunovs. Tsarina Maria, Boris's wife, was strangled, and Tsar Fedor was murdered "in a most loathsome way." The invaders spared only Ksenia, Boris's beautiful daughter — and only so that the pretender could make her his mistress. A few boyars then summoned Maria Nagaia, the real Dmitri's mother, from her convent to the Kremlin, and in an incredible scene she pronounced the imposter her long-lost son. She later admitted that she had lied because she feared for her life.

The next eight years — from 1605 to 1613 — are known as the Time of Troubles, a period during which the country was literally plunged into anarchy. The pretender quickly alienated his new subjects by inviting numerous Poles to Moscow, permitting them virtually to take over the capital, and barring Russian peasants from the Kremlin grounds. The boyars, ever inventive when their interests were at stake, claimed that the new tsar was not the real Dmitri after all and organized a Russian army, led by Prince Vasili Shuisky, to rout the Poles in the citadel. The False Dmitri tried to escape to organize a new army by jumping out of the palace window, but he injured himself as he landed, was apprehended by Shuisky's men, and was immediately killed. In May 1606 a crowd of nobles and commoners gathered in Red Square to proclaim Shuisky Tsar of Russia.

By this time conditions in the country had deteriorated to such an extent that the new ruler found it impossible to maintain order. Violent class warfare raged in several regions of the state, brigandage was rampant, and both the Poles and the Swedes intervened in Russian affairs. During the next two years a score of new pretenders appeared, all of whom rallied some support among disaffected Muscovites of various social classes.

In 1607 the cause of the second pretender — the most successful of the lot — presented the Polish Catholic clergy with an amusing moral dilemma. They sought to bolster his claim to the Muscovite throne by arranging for Marina Mniszech, wife of the False Dmitri, to acknowledge him as her husband, but this second imposter was so physically unappealing that when Marina saw him she purportedly shuddered. Nevertheless, she was eventually persuaded to overcome her revulsion, a change of heart occasioned in part by her ambition to be tsarina and in part by her father's desire to be close to the seat of power. Although the priests and her father seemed not the slightest bit disturbed by her lying about the pretender's identity, they could not suffer Marina to commit the mortal sin of cohabiting with a man they knew was not her husband. A public marriage would have exposed the entire scheme as a fraud, and the dilemma could only be resolved by means of a secret marriage ceremony.

Recognized by his "wife," the new pretender marched into Muscovy in June 1608 and encamped in Tushino, nine miles from the capital. There the "Brigand of Tushino," as he was nicknamed, set up a government and laid siege to Moscow. Two tsars now vied for supremacy, and many nobles who nurtured a grievance against Shuisky moved to the "second capital" to support the Brigand. At this time there emerged a sizable group of boyars — known as the *perelety* — who regularly shuttled back and forth between the two centers; the allegiance of the *perelety* at any particular moment depended on the attractiveness of the promises of privileges and land grants made by the "rulers." But the Brigand did not remain in Tushino for long. His relentless plundering of the countryside turned the people against him, and in December 1609 they drove him from the town. A few months later a Tatar officer killed him in revenge for his murder of the ruler of Kasimov.

To add to the confusion, a rebellious force deposed Shuisky in 1610 and offered the crown to Wladyslaw, son of King Sigismund of Poland, on the understanding that he would convert to Orthodoxy. According to the Russian Chronicles, Wladyslaw "was to be reborn to a new life, like a blind man who has recovered his eyesight." The only difficulty was that Sigismund wanted the crown for himself. He dispatched an army against Muscovy that captured Smolensk and then entrenched itself in the Kremlin after burning much of Moscow. At the same time the Swedes occupied Novgorod and offered one of their princes as a candidate for the throne. As one historian has put it, by 1611 the Muscovite state was in "universal and complete disruption."

Salvation came from an unexpected source. In Nizhni Novgorod, a well-to-do butcher and merchant named Kuzma Minin took it upon himself to form a national

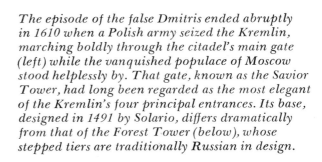

The episode of the false Dmitris ended abruptly in 1610 when a Polish army seized the Kremlin, marching boldly through the citadel's main gate (left) while the vanquished populace of Moscow stood helplessly by. That gate, known as the Savior Tower, had long been regarded as the most elegant of the Kremlin's four principal entrances. Its base, designed in 1491 by Solario, differs dramatically from that of the Forest Tower (below), whose stepped tiers are traditionally Russian in design.

movement to oust the enemy. A remarkable organizer and public-spirited citizen, he convinced the city commune to impose new taxes for the creation of an army of liberation. Other cities joined the effort, and many lesser nobles who had suffered from the chaos rushed to his support. Minin also had the good sense to call on the able Prince Dmitri Pozharsky to lead the army.

After four months of preparation, Minin and Pozharsky joined with a Cossack force headed by Prince Trubetskoi and advanced on the capital. Their army of 10,000 men faced Polish forces numbering 15,000, but the army of liberation cleverly invested the city for three months before launching its attack in October 1612. That assault gave them control of every section except the Kremlin, where the Poles continued to hold out. Cut off from supplies, the defenders could not hope to resist for long, and when the food shortage among the Poles became acute, they reportedly resorted to cannibalism. After five days they surrendered, and the critical stage of the struggle for liberation was over. The Russians have not forgotten the heroic efforts of Minin and Pozharsky; a memorial to them still stands at the edge of Red Square.

The next task was to reestablish authority in the country by finding a man whom the people would accept as sovereign. Early in 1613 a *zemski sobor* was convened, and after much wrangling the delegates settled on sixteen-year-old Michael Romanov, who was distantly related to the old dynasty. The family tie endowed Michael with the mantle of legitimacy, but the boyars who supported his election were also motivated by another consideration. Fedor Sheremetov revealed it in a private letter written at the time: "Let

us elect Misha [Michael] Romanov, he is young and still not wise, he'll be agreeable to us." Even though the assembly unanimously elected him tsar, Michael initially refused the honor because his mother felt he was too young to cope with the turbulent conditions in the country. Only after a delegation from the *zemski sobor* assured her that the nation stood ready to obey Michael and to end the civil strife did he agree to serve. On July 11, 1613, Michael was formally crowned in the Uspenski sobor, thus initiating a dynasty that was to rule Russia for three hundred years. (See genealogy, page 164.)

With rare exceptions, the Romanovs were undistinguished sovereigns. The three who dominated much of the seventeenth century — Michael, Alexis, and Fedor — demonstrated scant imagination as leaders. Nonetheless, under their aegis the country regained stability. The rulers took advantage of this period of relative calm by turning their attention once again to beautifying the Kremlin. In 1625 Christopher Halloway, an Englishman, built the upper stories of the Spasskaia (Savior) Tower. Rising high above the main entrance to the Kremlin, the tower is covered with frescoes that are a blend of Italian Renaissance ornamental work and motifs of Oriental origin. The name derives from the fact that an image of Christ is painted on the wall over the gate. At one time a decorative lantern hung in front of the gilded frame around the image, and it was customary to keep its candles burning both day and night. Additional towers were erected, among them the Tower of Patriarch Philaret in 1624 and the small Tsar Tower in 1680, and others were freshly decorated. Between 1642 and 1644 five icon masters

directed no fewer than a hundred painters in the embellishment of the vaults and walls of the Uspenski sobor with a new, if thoroughly conventional, decorative scheme.

Michael and Alexis took special interest in rebuilding the Granovitaia palata, or Palace of Facets, which had been almost completely demolished during the Polish occupation of the Kremlin. In the middle of the seventeenth century Alexis engaged a number of foreign craftsmen, many of them Polish, who introduced luxuries hitherto unknown in Russia. According to one account, "the walls were covered with gilded leather, the ceilings ornamented with precious metals, and new kinds of conveniences, doors and cupboards, bookcases and furniture from abroad, were installed." Flemish and Persian tapestries covered the walls of the state apartments in the renovated palace, and the ceiling of the formal dining room was painted to represent "with astronomical accuracy the solar system and the fixed stars."

Tsar Alexis also devoted many years to converting the spacious palace of the boyar Ilia Miloslavsky into a theater and place of amusement. Known as the Amusement Palace, this structure still exists, although it has undergone substantial changes during the past three centuries. Finally, between 1680 and 1690 a number of whimsical and somewhat effete gardens, balconies, stairways, and hanging gardens were added to the Kremlin grounds.

It would be misleading to mention only the constructive work of the first Romanovs in restoring political stability and promoting artistic endeavors, for their actions were also instrumental in provoking a reli-

Two years after its ignominious surrender to the Poles, the Kremlin was liberated by a nationalist army raised by a butcher named Minin and led by a veteran field commander named Prince Pozharsky. Their motley but zealous followers recaptured the city and citadel in 1612 after a three-month-long siege, and the grateful Muscovites eventually erected a statue in their honor in Red Square (left). When order was finally restored, a zemski sobor, or parliament, was convened to select a new tsar. After months of indecision, the council's choice fell upon sixteen-year-old Michael Romanov. A contemporary miniature (below) executed during Michael's reign shows a formal procession filing past the Palace of Facets (right) and the Red Stairway (center) on its way to the Cathedral of the Archangel (left).

In a display of unabashed pride in their craft and their city, Moscow's leading foundrymen began to cast the world's largest bell (near right) in a special pit in the Kremlin compound in 1733. The pouring alone took two years, and the great bell was still cooling in its pit when a fire swept the yard in 1737. Heated unevenly by the flames, the bell sundered and a wedge-shaped section of the lip broke off. Today deep fissures scar many of the bell's bas-reliefs, but the portrait of Tsar Alexei I (below) remains undamaged. A detail (far right) from the bow case of Alexei's father, Michael Romanov, shows Saint George slaying the dragon.

gious schism that led to both social convulsion and permanent discord within Russian Orthodoxy. The rift began in 1653 when Patriarch Nikon, then a favorite of Tsar Alexis, introduced some seemingly trivial reforms in religious ritual and texts. Nikon's purpose was as much political as spiritual: he hoped to bring the Russian liturgy and customs into conformity with those of Constantinople in order to facilitate the planned unification between Muscovy and the Ukraine, where the Church had remained faithful to old Greek practices. Thus, for example, he proposed that the spelling of Jesus, incorrectly inscribed in Muscovite texts, be amended; that in making the cross three rather than two fingers be used; that the Alleluia be chanted thrice instead of twice during services; and that religious processions move in the direction of the sun rather than counter to it.

Because of the low educational level of the Russian people and clergy, religious ritual mattered far more to them than dogma or substance. In their eyes the slightest deviation from established practices — such as the reforms advanced by Nikon — amounted to heresy. The archpriest Avvakum, who led the opposition to the changes, recalled his initial reaction to them: "We [the zealots of the church] gathered together to think it over. We saw that winter was about to overcome us. Our hearts became cold, and our legs trembled."

The opposition mounted a campaign against the reforms to which the patriarch and the government responded by urging their acceptance more ruthlessly than ever. Some of the zealots, including Avvakum, were exiled to Siberia, others were anathematized, and a feverish hunt was begun for icons that in any way

differed from the Byzantine model. Homes were searched for the offending images, which were then publicly destroyed, sometimes by the patriarch himself. By the 1660's the *Raskol,* or Great Schism, had torn the church asunder and left in its wake a group of dissenters who came to be known as *Raskolniki,* or Old Believers.

In the meantime, personal differences terminated the relationship between the patriarch Nikon and Tsar Alexis. The arrogant and impetuous manner of the patriarch, as well as his belief that ecclesiastical power supersedes the temporal, thoroughly alienated the tsar. At a church council that Alexis held in his Kremlin palace in 1666–67, he denounced Nikon for innumerable transgressions of Muscovite law and for offenses against the sovereign and the boyars. In a move that officially affirmed the supremacy of the secular ruler over the Church, the council deposed Nikon and banished him from Moscow. Yet the campaign for reform continued and was even intensified. The council formally cursed and anathematized all dissenters, and the tsar ordered that the tongues of two recalcitrant priests be cut out — a punishment then considered fitting for blasphemy. Such interference by the State in essentially ecclesiastical matters accelerated the process of totally subjugating the Russian Orthodox Church to temporal authorities.

The Old Believers, who felt that the State hampered the way to eternal salvation, turned increasingly to fanaticism. Many dissenters sank into such despair over the state of affairs that they became convinced that the end of the world was imminent. They proclaimed that the apocalypse would occur in 1666 or in 1669 — and when both years passed without catastrophe they forecast that the end would come in 1698. They even claimed to know precisely how the ultimate calamity would take place: "The sun would be eclipsed, the stars fall from the sky, the earth be burned up, and on the Day of Judgment the last trumpet blown by the Archangel would summon together the righteous and the unrighteous." Confident in the accuracy of their prophesy, many thought it senseless to remain on earth and risk being contaminated by heresy. As a result, between 1672 and 1691 there were thirty-seven horrifying mass immolations in which more than 20,000 dissenters voluntarily burned to death. In addition, the government burned many Old Believers at the stake, among them the archpriest Avvakum.

Far from unifying Russian Orthodoxy, as he had hoped, the reforms Nikon introduced generated irreconcilable conflicts among the people. It has been estimated that in 1880 there were some 13,000,000 dissenters — among them the Church's most devout members — out of a total population of about 90,000,000. Above all, the religious schism of the 1660's inaugurated the practice of governmental persecution of religious minorities — a practice that has remained virtually a permanent feature of Russian state policy until the present day.

In the troubled times of the mid-seventeenth century, Russia desperately needed a forceful, charismatic, and visionary leader — a man who could, through the sheer force of his personality, unite the warring factions of Russian society into a cohesive and politically potent whole. Muscovy was to find such a man in Peter I, son of Alexis by his second wife.

V
A Window to the West

Peter the Great's personality was so overwhelming and demonic, and his policies so novel and unsettling, that many of his subjects believed that he was neither an ordinary mortal nor the legitimate heir to the throne. In the eyes of the clergy, Peter embodied none other than the Antichrist who intended to lead the people into evil ways. A widely accepted legend held that the tsar was not of royal blood at all, but a usurper "born of a German outcast, and abandoned as a foundling." Shortly after his birth his mother, Tsarina Natalia Naryshkin, is alleged to have exclaimed in horror: "No son of mine art thou. Thou art a changeling."

Peter's great physical strength and extraordinary size alone — he was almost seven feet tall — seemed to proclaim to the world that he was no Romanov. In addition, his behavior did not conform to the standards expected of royalty. One can well imagine the consternation of the people at the spectacle of "a tsar who wore no crown, nor walked in purple, but, taking axe in hand, would thrust pipe between teeth, toil like a plain sailor, dress and smoke like a German, drink like a trooper, and swear and brawl like an officer of the Guards." Proud of his manual dexterity, he claimed to have mastered fourteen trades as well as surgery and dentistry. When courtiers and servants took sick they tried to conceal it from Peter, for if he thought that medical attention was needed, he would gather his instruments and offer his services. Among his personal belongings Peter left a sackful of teeth — testimony to his thriving dental practice.

Stories of Peter's sadistic behavior reached his people during the early years of his reign. It became known, for example, that he delighted in forcing all his guests, including the ladies, to drink their vodka straight — the way he liked it — and in large quantities. "Only the spiritual dignitaries," we are told, "turned not their faces from the fiery cup." Johann Korb, the secretary to the Austrian embassy in Moscow from 1698 to 1699, described a particularly gruesome incident at one of these festive occasions: "Boyar Golowin has, from his cradle, a natural horror of salad and vinegar; so the Czar directing Colonel Chambers to hold him tight, forced salad and vinegar into his mouth and nostrils, until the blood flowing from his nose succeeded his violent coughing."

Despite his monstrous eccentricities, Peter was determined to transform his country into a powerful and enlightened nation, and to root out ancient customs and traditions. His achievement was substantial, but the cost was enormous: Peter's endless military campaigns drained Russia's resources, and his attempts at Westernization shocked the hidebound masses, most of whom were genuinely distressed by the tsar's policies. Although he was in many respects a sensitive person, Peter had little understanding of human nature, and it never occurred to him that compulsion was not the most effective way to persuade an ignorant and superstitious people of the desirability of rapid change. Indeed, he held the simple-minded notion that "the more ignorant a country, the easier it would be to educate it" — and his primary method of education was coercion. In essence his failing as a ruler stemmed from the fact that "he was better with inanimate objects than with people, whom he treated as if they were merely tools." Consequently he could not grasp the obvious contradiction between his attempts to "civilize Russia with the Knout" and "bind together a nation lacking in cohesion." It is no wonder that desperate Muscovites of all classes asked themselves time and again: "Can this be the *rightful* tsar?"

Actually, there is no doubt about Peter's legitimacy. Nor can any mystery be attached to the development of his eccentric character. Peter's personality, like that of Ivan the Terrible (whom he greatly admired), was molded largely by his traumatic childhood experiences. His mother, Natalia Naryshkin, was the second wife of Tsar Alexis, the second Romanov ruler. From the moment she moved into the Kremlin early in 1671, Natalia had been obliged to contend with the animosity of the Miloslavskys, relatives of Alexis's first wife, who had died in 1669. The Miloslavskys, fearful of losing favor at court, had encouraged the tsar to marry some other member of their family, and they resented his failure to do so. Furthermore, several of Alexis's children disliked having a stepmother who was younger than they. As a result Peter, who was born in 1672, spent his first four years in this tense atmosphere. The situation was compounded in 1676 when Alexis died; Fedor, Peter's half brother, succeeded to the throne, and the Miloslavskys took control of the Kremlin.

The new ruler was sickly, however, and his death stirred a serious crisis over the succession. Peter's other half brother, Ivan, was entitled to the throne, but everyone knew that he could not possibly govern. Aside from being mentally deficient, he was virtually blind and suffered from a speech defect and epilepsy. The nobles therefore ignored his claim and proclaimed the ten-year-old Peter tsar — on the understanding that his mother would act as regent during his minority.

But the Miloslavskys refused to be shunted aside so easily. They exploited the disaffection among the *streltsy*, who had genuine grievances about the maltreatment they received at the hands of their officers, by asserting that the Naryshkins intended to oppress the musketeers even more severely. The aroused *streltsy* organized a demonstration in the streets of Moscow and gathered support by shouting: "The Naryshkins have murdered the Tsarevich Ivan! To the Kremlin! The Naryshkins wish to kill all the royal family! To arms! Punish the traitors! Save the tsar!"

The *streltsy* stormed through the Kremlin gates and ran wild for three days, committing senseless murders and wreaking wanton destruction. Some of the most dramatic scenes took place on the Red Stairway, the striking entrance to the royal palace that was covered with scarlet carpets on festive occasions. In the hope of calming the *streltsy*, Natalia courageously appeared at the top of the stairs together with Peter and Ivan. But even though it was clear that the Miloslavskys had not been harmed, the soldiers refused to end their rebellion. They demanded that the tsarina hand over to them her foster father, the aged Artaman Matveiev. When she complied, they hurled him into the square, where he was cut to pieces in full view of Peter — who watched the gory proceedings without betraying a trace of emotion.

The *streltsy* then invaded the palace and dragged several Naryshkins (including two of Natalia's brothers) and other powerful boyars into the square for another round of massacre. They cut the hands and feet off one of the tsarina's brothers, chopped his feet into bits and trampled them into the mud. All told, more

than a dozen people were murdered. The ghastly disorders came to an end only when it was agreed to make Sofia Miloslavsky, Peter's half sister, regent, and both Peter and Ivan co-tsars — a novel arrangement that Sofia claimed was divinely inspired. After this Miloslavsky triumph Natalia and Peter moved to the village of Preobrazhensk, about three miles from the center of Moscow.

To remind future generations of their achievements, the *streltsy* compelled the government to erect a column in Red Square on which were inscribed the names of the massacre's victims and their alleged crimes. A Dutch resident in Moscow at the time strongly endorsed the project, considering it a "good lesson and warning to the bribetakers who have caused so much disorder." Peter did not need a monument to remind him of the horrors of 1682. The events of that year remained indelibly inscribed in his mind and seem to have bred within him a moral callousness that became ever more pronounced as he matured. Moreover, for the rest of his life Peter disliked the Kremlin intensely.

At Preobrazhensk Natalia preoccupied herself with dreams of revenge against the Miloslavskys and left Peter to his own devices. The lad received a formal education of only the most rudimentary kind, but he was highly intelligent, had a fine memory and remarkable curiosity, especially in regard to things mechanical, and therefore educated himself in those fields that appealed to him. Gifted with his hands, he quickly acquired a certain proficiency in carpentry, masonry, and metal work. Sailing and boatbuilding also intrigued him, but his greatest passion was to "play" with

live soldiers. At the age of eleven he procured guns, lead, powder, and shot for his soldiers and within a few years built his own six-hundred-man army — the nucleus of the future imperial guards. Nothing gave him greater pleasure than to conduct military maneuvers, some of which were sufficiently true to life to leave a sizable number of wounded and killed in their wake.

One night during the summer of 1689 Peter received the alarming news that Sofia planned to have herself crowned tsarina and that she had dispatched several companies of *streltsy* to arrest him. Without bothering to get dressed, Peter leaped on a horse and raced off to the monastery-fortress of Holy Trinity, forty miles from Preobrazhensk. Sofia, who had in fact lost popularity among the musketeers, found herself unable to mobilize them in support of her seizure of power; Peter and his soldier regiments managed to crush the plot without firing a shot. He sent Sofia to a convent, exiled some of her advisers and had one of them hanged, and deposed Ivan as co-tsar. But the young tsar was not yet ready to assume the burdens of power. He allowed his mother to run the government until she died in 1694, and only then did he begin to take a serious interest in political affairs.

In the meantime, Peter married Eudoxia Lopukhina, whom he never loved and whom he deserted after two months. He much preferred the company of foreigners in the so-called "German suburb" that lay between Preobrazhensk and the Kremlin. Between 1689 and 1694 he spent much of his time there with Dutch and English merchants, whom he pumped for information about the latest mechanical devices and political developments in Europe. It was there that his interest in the West was first seriously aroused, and it was there that he became further estranged from his wife by taking as his mistress a commoner, the daughter of a German wine merchant.

The death of Peter's mother forced him to direct his sole attention to ruling the country at last. His most distinctive trait as sovereign was his activism; in foreign as well as domestic affairs he continually initiated new policies. Although not a profound thinker, he had the capacity to grasp difficult problems and devise solutions. His prodigious energy and drive are perhaps best exemplified by the fact that he rarely stayed in any one place more than three months; he insisted on being at the center of the action, whether it was the battlefield, the negotiating table, the torture chamber, or a shipyard. He made heavy demands on himself and his people, but not primarily for reasons of personal glorification. Unlike his predecessors, he did not identify himself with the state but considered himself its first servant, and he justified his exacting policies on the grounds that they promoted the interests of Russia. In view of these superhuman exertions, as well as his frequent debaucheries, it is not surprising that he developed a nervous twitch on the left side of his face that sometimes was distorted into a grimace.

Peter first demonstrated his eccentricity as a ruler in 1697, when he visited the West, an unprecedented undertaking for a Muscovite monarch. One of his purposes was to seek allies among European kings for a military crusade against Turkey, but his major reason was to study Western industrial techniques, especially shipbuilding, and to engage skilled craftsmen and naval officers to send back to Russia. Because the tsar wanted to feel free to work in the industrial establishments he visited, he traveled under the name of Peter Mikhailov, an alias that deceived virtually no one.

Peter's five months in Holland were filled with diverse activities: he inspected factories, workshops, hospitals, schools, military installations, and an observatory. In each place he asked detailed questions, and whenever possible he took part in the work, at least for a short while. He even attended lectures by famous anatomists and insisted on watching them dissect cadavers. On one such occasion he saw "the body of a child so beautifully laid out as to seem still to be alive" and, with a smile, "bent down and kissed the infant." On another, he noticed that some members of his retinue were repelled by the sight of a dead body, whereupon he "bade them sever the corpse's muscles with their teeth." In the town of Zaandam Peter startled the townspeople by working in a shipyard as a common carpenter. The small house he occupied there for a week has been preserved as a museum.

Early in 1698 he moved on to England where, after a cordial welcome by King William III, he again made the rounds, including a visit to the House of Lords. On hearing the interpreter's report on the debates, he declared: "When subjects thus do speak the truth unto the Sovereign, it is goodly hearing. Let us learn in this of the English." This was mere talk, of course, but Peter was serious about studying English methods of shipbuilding, and for this purpose he settled for a few weeks in Deptford, which was close to a government dockyard.

Although he applied himself to this project with cus-

Peter I's extraordinary and utterly unprecedented decision to make a grand tour of the West in 1697 shocked his hidebound boyars and intrigued the courts of Western Europe, where the young tsar's seven-foot frame, rough manner, and crude disguise were greeted with a mixture of curiosity and contempt. Lingering a full five months in Holland (left), Peter acquired a thorough understanding of modern shipbuilding techniques — lessons he put into practice upon his return to Russia a year later. Peter's model navy is the subject of the contemporary engraving below.

tomary zeal, Peter did not neglect his private pleasures in Deptford, as the dismayed owner of the house he occupied soon discovered. The royal retinue broke much of the furniture and ripped down the curtains during a succession of riotous parties. In addition, the pictures on the walls were used for target practice and the well-kept gardens were converted into a drill ground.

Predictably, Peter made an unfavorable impression on the English. Bishop Burnet, who saw him several times, stated that the tsar "seems designed by nature rather to be a ship-carpenter, than a great prince." His meetings with Peter also prompted the bishop to reflect that "God moves in a mysterious way his wonders to perform. . . . I could not but adore the depth of the providence of God, that had raised up such a furious man to so absolute an authority over so great a part of the world. . . . Man seems a very contemptible thing in the sight of God," the bishop concluded, "while such a person as the Czar has such multitudes put as it were under his feet, exposed to his restless jealousy and savage temper."

In the spring Peter returned to the Continent, arriving in Vienna in May 1698. He intended to proceed to Venice, but news of another conspiracy fomented by his half sister and a new rebellion led by four *streltsy* regiments caused him to change his plans. By this time he had been abroad for fifteen months, and he rightly feared that if he prolonged his absence he might lose power. In any case, he had every reason to be satisfied with his accomplishments, for in addition to improving substantially his technical knowledge he had recruited 750 specialists in naval affairs, engineering, and medicine and purchased an impressive array of military supplies. Without further delay, therefore, he hurried back to the Kremlin.

Within a day of his return Peter shocked his Muscovite subjects by personally cutting off the beards of leading nobles as well as the long sleeves of their surcoats. Somewhat later he issued decrees requiring everyone except peasants and clergymen to appear clean-shaven and wear Hungarian or German dress on pain of having to pay an annual tax. Another measure that disturbed the people was the Westernization of the Russian calendar: the New Year was to be celebrated on January 1 instead of September 1, and beginning with the new century the years would be counted not from the presumed date of the world's creation but from that of Christ's birth. Thus, the year 7208 became 1700.

Peter reasoned that only by means of these seemingly trivial innovations could the Russian people rid themselves of their backward Asiatic customs and become energetic, enterprising citizens. The change in attire would also bring practical benefits, for it would give the Russians greater freedom of bodily movement. As the tsar told a group of officers who still wore long sleeves: "See, these things are in your way. You are safe nowhere with them. At one moment you upset a glass, then you dip them in the sauce. Get gaiters made of them."

The people, especially the lower classes, did not take kindly to Peter's reforms. The beard in particular contributed significantly to preserving the "image of God" in which they believed man to be made. They thought that by shaving it off they would be reduced to the level of cats and dogs and would court eternal

Having consolidated his power, Peter moved swiftly and ruthlessly against his implacable foes, the musketeers known as streltsy. *His memories of the* streltsy *rebellion of 1682 — during which several members of his mother's family were butchered in Red Square — were vivid, and the tower that the* streltsy *had erected to commemorate the slaughter was still standing (left). Peter's reprisals were brutal but effective: in the space of two years, some 1,200* streltsy *were executed in Red Square (right).*

damnation. The depth of feeling on the subject is amusingly illustrated by the experience of an English visitor, Captain John Perry. The Englishman teased a worker on the loss of his beard and asked what he had done with it:

> Upon which he put his hand in his Bosom and pull'd it out, and shew'd it to me; farther telling me, that when he came home, he would lay it up and have it put in his Coffin and buried along with him, that he might be able to give an Account of it to St. Nicholas, when he came to the other World; and that all his Brothers (meaning his Fellow-workmen who had been shaved that Day) had taken the same Care.

Another incident makes the same point. In 1705 two young men approached the Metropolitan of Rostov for advice, complaining that they would sooner lose their heads than their beards. The prelate countered with a rhetorical question: "Which of the twain, I pray you, would grow again the more easily?"

A further cause for dismay among Peter's subjects was his brutal treatment of the rebellious *streltsy*. Peter lost no time in initiating extensive investigations, but no one seemed able or willing to answer all the questions to his satisfaction. Consequently he began to doubt everyone's loyalty and decided indiscriminately to massacre suspects in Red Square. According to some accounts, the tsar himself participated in the executions. On one occasion he is said to have cut off eighty-four rebel heads with a sword. In all, over twelve hundred *streltsy* were exterminated, and many of their bodies were left in the streets of Moscow for the entire winter in order to terrorize the population. As an added precaution against future conspiracies, Peter

forced his half sister Sofia to shave her head and take the veil.

Despite Peter's indisputable cruelty, it would be a mistake to view him as a completely heartless man. He could be thoughtful and compassionate, even toward people who occasionally neglected their work, a failing he normally found difficult to tolerate. Ivan Nepluev, superintendent of docks, recalled an incident that reveals these traits. One morning Nepluev overslept and, certain that the tsar would punish him severely, dreaded going to work. But instead of reporting in sick, his first impulse, he decided to risk the ruler's wrath by telling the truth. "I am already here," said Peter on seeing Nepluev. "It is my fault," replied the superintendent. "I stayed up too late last night making merry." To his surprise, the tsar put his hand on Nepluev's shoulder and said: "Thank you for the truth; God will forgive you; there is nobody who has not sinned."

Peter was devoted to his friends, and he was capable of public displays of emotion. In 1699, for example, at the funeral of his favorite, General Lefort, Peter made no effort to conceal his sorrow. According to Korb, "When the moment for removing the body came, the grief and affection of the Czar . . . was manifest to everybody, for the Czar shed tears most abundantly, and in the sight of all the vast crowd of people who were assembled on account of the solemn ceremony, he gave his last kiss to the corpse." But Peter could never muster sympathy or mercy for political opponents. He was unquestionably a tyrant who early in his reign resolved to make it clear that he would insist on absolute obedience to his word. To be sure,

local rebellions — some quite massive — placed this principle in question from time to time, but after 1698 his authority was sufficiently secure to allow him to concentrate his energies on military affairs and domestic reform, his chief interests.

Russia waged war, usually at Peter's instigation, during most of his thirty-six-year reign. In fact, in the period from 1689 to 1725, the country enjoyed only one full year and thirteen isolated months of peace. Determined to bring about the political unification of all the Russian people and to rectify his nation's exposed frontiers in the south and west, Peter became entangled in military conflicts with Sweden, Turkey, and finally Persia. Occasionally he suffered painful defeats, but on balance Russia emerged from the encounters a far stronger nation.

His most costly and most rewarding war, the one with Sweden, lasted from 1700 to 1721 and is known as the Great Northern War. Sweden was then one of the leading European powers, and until 1718 her armies were commanded by the brilliant and daring strategist King Charles XII. When Peter defeated the Swedes in 1709 in the famous battle of Poltava, he not only saved Russia from invasion but propelled the country into the forefront of European diplomacy. At the war's end twelve years later, when the treaty of Nystad was signed, Sweden was thoroughly humbled. Russia controlled the Baltic coast from Riga to Viborg, having confirmed possession of the provinces of Livonia, Estonia, Ingria, and a part of Karelia. Thus consolidated, Russia's position as a major European power has survived to the present day.

Peter feted the victory in grand style. For seven days and nights, he compelled the leading nobles to remain in the senate building to celebrate. He himself, "half-demented with joy at having brought the struggle to a successful issue, and forgetful alike of years and gout . . . danced upon the tables [and] sang songs." Then, allegedly in response to the urgent pleas of the senate, he agreed to accept the titles of Emperor and Father of the Country.

These festivities took place not in the Kremlin, but in Peter's new capital, St. Petersburg, which he called his "paradise" and "darling." Three considerations prompted him to build a city in the swamps at the head of the Gulf of Finland near the mouth of the Neva River: his love for the sea, a desire to perpetuate his memory, and hatred for the Kremlin. Beginning in 1703 and spanning the next twenty years, the royal coffers were ransacked to create this "great window for Russia to look out at Europe" or, as some have called it, Russia's "window to the West." The conquests ratified by the treaty of Nystad gave Peter the territorial security for his capital that he had so persistently sought.

On the grounds that every mason was needed in St. Petersburg, the tsar forbade even the slightest repairs on the stone buildings in Moscow, which gradually fell into disrepair. Because of the cold, damp climate around St. Petersburg, Peter had to rely heavily on forced labor to complete the grueling task of erecting the new capital. There was much grumbling among the workers, who suffered from various illnesses — especially dysentery — but Peter would not be deterred. Some historians state that construction of the new capital claimed 10,000 lives a year for twenty years. This is probably an exaggeration, but no one questions the

The Peterine Reforms were a subject of special interest to Vasili Surikov, the foremost exponent of the late-nineteenth-century school of Russian realism. In The Morning of the Streltsy Execution *(below), a study of the carnage that filled Red Square in the early 1700's, Surikov has cast Peter the Great in the heroic mold. Mounted upon a white stallion and silhouetted against the Kremlin's crenelated walls, Peter (below right) remains physically as well as spiritually aloof from the doomed streltsy. In sharp contrast, the enameled miniature at right captures Peter and his family in a thoroughly domestic moment.*

deaths of many thousands in the endeavor — nor is there any doubt that the cost ran into millions of rubles, for Peter had longed for an imposing capital and was prepared to spend accordingly. He engaged the distinguished French architect Jean Baptiste Leblon and other Western experts to design the city and its palaces, and paid them all extraordinary sums. Leblon's chief work was the tsar's country residence at Peterhof. With its formal gardens, terraces, fountains, and cascades it resembles the palace and gardens at Versailles, whose grandeur Peter doubtless hoped to reproduce.

By 1714 the building of St. Petersburg had progressed sufficiently for the senate to move there, and in 1718 the ministries settled in the city, which became the official capital, a status it retained for two centuries. Some government offices remained in the Kremlin, and from time to time Russian rulers visited the ancient capital — usually to pray in the cathedrals or to attend coronation ceremonies — but it no longer enjoyed its former preeminence.

In his relentless drive to create a powerful and prosperous state Peter increasingly came to realize the necessity of modernizing his country. He did not initiate change as a result of philosophical commitment, but rather because of the exigencies of war, which compelled him to undertake one reform after another. In the end hardly an institution remained unaffected — and the foundations of modern Russia had been laid.

Peter initially took rather novel measures to bolster the country's military strength. He built a sizable navy — a significant innovation, for Russia had never before aspired to being a naval power — and that eight-hundred-ship fleet contributed substantially to Sweden's

defeat, although it should be noted that the navy did not long survive Peter as an effective force. More lasting was his creation of a standing army that by 1725 consisted of roughly 200,000 troops. Its effectiveness was enhanced by Peter's insistence on rigorous, up-to-date training, the use of the most modern weapons, and the hiring of foreign officers. The construction of the Arsenal Building in the Kremlin, begun in 1702 and completed in 1736, symbolized the tsar's determination to remodel the army.

None of Peter's ambitious projects could be implemented without money, which was always in short supply. From 1705 to 1707, for example, the government's expenditures exceeded its income by 20 per cent. To cope with this problem, Peter repeatedly overhauled the system of taxation, constantly increasing the burden on the common people, and in 1724 he imposed a soul tax on all males of the nonprivileged classes. This tax, which in effect extended serfdom by abolishing the legal distinctions between serfs and other groups of bondsmen, was a fiscal triumph: direct taxes now brought in 4,500,000 rubles instead of 1,800,000. By granting various exemptions and privileges Peter also stimulated the development of industry during the first decades of the eighteenth century, but despite initial gains many of these enterprises went out of business by mid-century due to the inferior grade of their products.

Finally, Peter reorganized the administrative structure of the state. He granted urban communities a degree of self-government, replaced the sluggish central departments with Swedish "colleges," and established a senate that served as the highest judicial and

administrative organ and occasionally exercised legislative authority. To promote greater efficiency, he also divided the country into provinces, which in turn were subdivided into districts. In 1721 he completed the process of subjugating the Church to the State by substituting for the patriarchate the "Holy Governing Senate," a body of ten men appointed by the tsar. The chief procurator, whose job it was to supervise the work of the synod, was also appointed by the tsar. It is noteworthy that in formulating many of these reforms Peter relied on the advice of Gottfried Leibnitz, the German mathematician and philosopher who supplied the tsar with numerous concrete suggestions in return for a handsome annual retainer.

Although they were by no means fully successful and many left their mark primarily on the privileged classes, the Petrine reforms are generally considered to have raised the quality of government in Russia. Their very durability — some lasted as long as two centuries — supports this conclusion. In addition, it was Peter who placed the idea of Westernization on the agenda of Russian historical development. Henceforth the value of this idea, more than any other, would be debated by those Russians who speculated about their country's destiny.

Much as he prided himself on his accomplishments, Peter was constantly anguished by one question that he was never able to answer to his own satisfaction: Would he be succeeded by a man capable of carrying on his work? His rightful heir, Alexis, born to Eudoxia in 1690, turned out to be lazy and totally indifferent to affairs of state. Peter himself had overseen the tsarevich's education, but his counsel had had little ef-

fect on Alexis, who preferred drinking to more serious activities. In fact, Alexis admitted to Catherine I, Peter's second wife: "I have let business slide and am an idler." Peter berated Alexis for acting "like a young bird holding up its mouth to be fed," but to no avail. On the contrary, the more his father reproached him, the more Alexis resisted and turned his attention to trivialities. Their relationship deteriorated into one of open antagonism between "tormentor and tormented."

When Alexis grew to manhood, he infuriated his father by sympathizing with the "long beards," Peter's name for the priests who opposed his reformist policies. Then word reached the tsar that Alexis had been in touch with Eudoxia, who still yearned to avenge herself on Peter for having abandoned her. This news, together with his own chronic illnesses, brought the question of the succession to the fore in Peter's mind. His second wife had borne him only daughters, and he had no confidence in their ability to govern the country. He therefore reasoned that his only alternative was to have it out with the indolent and rebellious Alexis. The ensuing showdown was nearly as macabre as the altercation between Ivan the Terrible and his heir had been.

In a formal "Declaration to My Son," issued in the fall of 1715, the tsar criticized Alexis for his sloth and threatened to deprive him of the succession, "as one may cut off a useless member. . . . Whereas I do not spare my own life for my country and the welfare of my people, why should I spare you who do not render yourself worthy of either? I would rather choose to transmit them to a worthy stranger than to my own unworthy son." In reply Alexis confessed that he did

St. Petersburg, which Peter the Great called his "paradise," was little more than a marshy river delta when the tsar decided to relocate Russia's capital there. A century later, the glittering metropolis that Peter envisioned had taken tangible shape along a series of quays. This nineteenth-century panorama shows (left to right) the Marble Palace, Hermitage, Winter Palace, and Port of the Admiralty.

not think himself fit to govern and renounced his claim to the throne. "I put my children in your hands," he continued, "and as for myself, I desire nothing of you but a bare maintenance during my life, leaving the whole to your consideration and your will."

Peter refused to take his son's renunciation seriously. "Can one rely on your oaths," he asked, "when one sees that you have a hardened heart?" Peter could finally afford to be so demanding, for late in 1715 Catherine had at last given birth to a boy. He added the stipulation that Alexis either change his mode of conduct or immediately become a monk, apparently so as to prevent the young man from changing his mind about the renunciation. "I cannot be easy on your account, especially now that my health begins to decay. On the sight therefore of this letter, answer me upon it either in writing or by word of mouth. If you fail to do it, I will use you as a malefactor."

Once again Alexis yielded, but when Peter heard that his son had agreed to enter a monastery, he inexplicably told him to think it over and reach a final decision in six months. This change of mind totally confused Alexis, who continued his life of leisure and amusement. After seven months had passed he received another missive from his father, this one ordering him to join the tsar in Copenhagen for a new campaign against Sweden or immediately become a monk. By this time, however, Alexis's backbone had stiffened: he gave the impression of preparing for the trip to Copenhagen, but instead he fled to Vienna and then to Naples, where he lived with his mistress, a Finnish peasant girl.

Peter was doubly enraged because the Holy Roman Emperor, whose relations with the tsar were already

rocky, seemed to be protecting Alexis. Anxious to secure his son's return to Russia at all costs, Peter promised him a full and unconditional pardon and the opportunity to live in peace with his mistress on one of his estates. In February 1718, Alexis returned — and a few days thereafter Peter reneged on his promises. He declared that he would pardon his son only if he named the people who had helped him flee to Vienna and again renounced his right to the throne.

During the next few months Peter ordered the arrest, investigation, and torture of all those suspected of being sympathetic to Alexis. A gloomy mood pervaded St. Petersburg. "Innumerable accusations have given a sinister aspect to this capital," reported a French diplomat early in 1718; "it is as if the place was visited by a plague; everyone is either an accuser or an accused." Even Eudoxia and the Bishop of Rostov were subjected to humiliating inquiries, but no incriminating evidence could be found. Nonetheless, the bishop was broken on the wheel, and Eudoxia was eventually banished to a remote convent.

Alexis himself was interrogated seven times and, at his father's behest, tortured twice. On the second occasion, after having received twenty-five strokes of the knout, the tsarevich abjectly confessed to having conspired to ascend the throne illegally.

Actually, there is scant evidence to support the charge that Alexis had gone abroad to organize a coup d'état. Yet it is true that he had become a symbol to those who could no longer endure Peter's tyranny, his excessive taxes, and his reckless wars. Peter probably dealt with his own son as cruelly as he did in order to discredit the entire opposition. At any rate, he eventu-

More mellow in appearance (left) but no mellower in spirit, Peter entered the last decade of his life determined to ensure the succession of his line. The defection of one son and the death of another defeated Peter's purpose, however, and exposed the nation to another bitter power struggle. The vacuum created by Peter's death — one that was belatedly and inadequately filled by his niece Anne — is indicated by the contemporary woodcut at right, which is captioned "The mice bury the cat."

ally summoned a council of 127 high officials to pass judgment on Alexis. With "afflicted hearts and full of tears," the dignitaries condemned the tsarevich to death — and before Peter had a chance to confirm or reject the sentence, Alexis died in the fortress of saints Peter and Paul in St. Petersburg, apparently from wounds inflicted by his torturers. The government announced that he had succumbed to apoplexy, but it was widely believed that he had been murdered. Three days after the tsarevich's death Peter celebrated Alexis's saint's day by giving a lavish party that was described as "particularly gay."

As fate would have it, Alexis's demise only compounded the problem of the succession. In May 1719, Peter's surviving son died at the age of three, and the tsar was again left to ponder the future of his realm. In 1722 Peter abolished the existing rules of succession and decreed that henceforth the incumbent could appoint his heir. For some reason Peter himself failed to do so, and the upshot was that after his death the succession became a subject of precisely the sort of passionate dispute that he had hoped to forestall.

The tsar began having convulsions fairly frequently after 1720, and he also suffered excruciating pain from strangury and stones; but despite his agonies Peter refused to slow down or reduce his indulgence in sexual pleasures. One of his doctors even remarked that the tsar's "failings . . . principally, if not solely, arose from his inclination to the fair sex." One of Peter's close friends also believed that he exerted himself excessively, or at least indiscriminately: "In short, for a king he was as little elegant as expensive in his amours: as in things of the highest moment, so in this he acted

according to his inclinations without any regard to forms." There is evidence that he suffered from a chronic venereal disease, which would have further weakened his general condition.

In November 1724, while on an outing at sea, Peter caught sight of a shipwreck. With characteristic impetuosity, he jumped into the ice-cold water and labored to rescue the soldiers on the boat. This rash gesture precipitated an illness from which the fifty-three-year-old tsar did not recover. After suffering from a cold and high fever for several weeks, Peter died on February 8, 1725. Shortly afterward a woodcut was circulated depicting the burial. It bore the caption: "The mice bury the cat." The woodcut accurately expressed the mood of despair that had gripped the people of Muscovy, a despair that augured ill for the future of Russia, a land destined once again to suffer a period of turbulence.

VI
Enlightened Empress—or Autocrat?

I have been told that I was not welcomed very joyfully when I first appeared because a son was expected," Catherine the Great recorded in the opening paragraph of her memoirs. Her mother "only tolerated" her and frequently scolded her "severely and vehemently, and not always justly." As a youngster Catherine was repeatedly told that because she was ugly she should "strive for inward virtues and intelligence . . . for inward excellence." Her governess took pains to see to it that she always appeared in a favorable light before her parents, and this imposed unrealistic demands upon the child. "So it came about," Catherine confessed, "that I was rather devious for my tender years." When she grew up, one historian has stated, she was always "conscious of being on a stage, . . . acting first and foremost for show. . . . For her an act's setting and effect mattered more than either the act itself or the act's results." She also became fiercely ambitious, as if determined to prove that the family's disappointment that she had been born a girl had been a monumental mistake.

Only conditions as chaotic as those at the Russian court in the mid-eighteenth century could have made it possible for an obscure German princess from the duchy of Anhalt-Zerbst — such was Catherine's lineage — to realize her innermost ambition, to become the ruler of a major power. For nearly forty years after Peter the Great's death in 1725, Russia was ruled by thoroughly undistinguished sovereigns (see genealogy, page 164). Most of them succeeded to the throne as a result of palace revolutions in which the Corps of Guards played the decisive role. Intrigue, plots, and corruption prevailed while favorites — often foreigners

— administered the country. Indeed, it has been said that during the reigns of Empress Anne and her successor, Elizabeth, "lovers ruled Russia."

Unhappily, the major concern of these female sovereigns was their private amusement, which often assumed bizarre forms. Anne, who occupied the throne from 1730 to 1740, behaved in a particularly strange manner. During her reign, according to Florinsky, "the imperial residences were filled not only with animals and birds, especially those trained in the performance of tricks, but also with giants and dwarfs, hunchbacks and cripples, beggars and fools, while a large retinue of women, especially selected for their ability to chatter, spent hours spinning stories for the empress's entertainment." In 1740 she amused herself by organizing an elaborate wedding ceremony in which Prince A. M. Golitsyn, scion of one of Russia's most illustrious families, was married to a "Kalmyk woman of outstanding ugliness" in a "mansion built of ice."

Empress Elizabeth, who ruled from 1741 to 1762, was not much of an improvement. The daughter of Peter the Great, she suffered a terrible disappointment in 1727 when her fiancé, the Bishop of Lübeck, died shortly before the day they were to be wed. Elizabeth's grief was apparently genuine, but even so it is hard to think of her as the devoted wife of a clergyman, for with a single-mindedness reminiscent of her father's, she lived life to the fullest. In fact, she conducted herself so scandalously that the Spanish ambassador in St. Petersburg was moved to remark that the empress "shamelessly indulged in practices which would have made blush even the least modest person." Her preoccupation with amorous adventures left Elizabeth little time for other activities, and Russian statesmen and foreign diplomats were forever seeking an opportune moment to speak to her about political affairs or to persuade her to sign important documents. A major exception was her interest in architecture, which led her to commission the distinguished Italian architect Bartolomeo Rastrelli to build the first true imperial residence — the Winter Palace — in St. Petersburg. (Peter the Great had been content to live in a notably unpretentious structure in the city.)

In her favor it must also be said that Elizabeth took seriously the question of the succession. As she had no children, she invited the son of her sister Anne to come to Russia to prepare himself for the crown. The boy, whose name was Peter, had been born in 1728 to Anne and her husband, the Duke of Holstein. Anne died when Peter was only a few weeks old, and as a result his upbringing had devolved completely upon his father. When the duke himself died thirteen years later, Peter made the long journey to St. Petersburg. He arrived knowing only the German language and German customs, but within a year of his arrival he converted to Orthodoxy and accepted Russia as his home.

Having handpicked her immediate successor, Empress Elizabeth next sought to provide for her family's permanent retention of the crown. To that end she began to consider a bride for the future Peter III — and in 1744 she settled on Sophia Augusta Frederica of Anhalt-Zerbst, whose father, a petty German prince serving as the governor of Stettin, was delighted by the prospect of so brilliant a match. Mother and daughter eagerly undertook the arduous trip to Russia, and after the fifteen-year-old girl had been converted to Orthodoxy and rebaptized Catherine, she was married to Peter in 1745 in a glittering ceremony in the Church of Our Lady of Kazan in St. Petersburg. The bride wore a robe of cloth of silver and a jeweled Russian tiara. Empress Elizabeth, wishing to appear sophisticated, studied the elaborate celebrations of royal weddings in the West, especially at Versailles, and then proceeded to give gay parties such as had never before been known either in Moscow or St. Petersburg.

It was destined to be a disastrous union. Indeed, one can scarcely imagine two people more ill-suited to each other. Catherine was serious, intelligent, somewhat intellectually inclined, strong-willed, energetic — and, above all, ambitious. By contrast, Peter was sickly, dull, stubborn, and "phenomenally ignorant." He never matured intellectually, an historian has noted: "Grave matters he viewed jejunely; jejune matters he treated with the gravity of an adult." He knew no greater pleasure than to play with his dolls and toy soldiers, amusements that continued to preoccupy him even after his marriage. His one cultural accomplishment, playing the fiddle, could not be appreciated by Catherine, who was tone deaf; but those in a position to judge her husband's performances could testify to her good fortune in this instance. Physically, Peter was unprepossessing. In 1742 the English ambassador in St. Petersburg reported that "he looks very puny and he is not taller at fourteen than the generality of children . . . at ten." Additionally, as an adolescent he contracted smallpox which left his face disfigured.

Even during their courtship Catherine entertained serious doubts about the likelihood of their enjoying a happy marriage; from the start Peter struck her as

childish and boring. Furthermore, she was understandably disturbed by the fact that "we never used between us the language of tenderness; it was surely not my business to bring it into use, my modesty would not have allowed that even if I had felt so inclined, and my natural pride was sufficient to prevent my taking the first steps." It apparently did not occur to Peter to take those steps, a failure that did not dispose Catherine in his favor. For as she observed in her memoirs, "no matter how well brought up a maiden may be, she always likes to hear words of flattery and tenderness, especially from one to whom she may listen without blushing." Nonetheless, Catherine gave no thought to withdrawing from the match. She was disinclined to displease her mother, who strongly favored the marriage — and she had a compelling reason of her own, which she bluntly admitted: "I believe in truth . . . that the Russian crown meant more to me than he."

Peter and Catherine's lavish wedding ceremony was followed by ten days of festivities, but if we can trust Catherine's memoirs, a pall descended on the gaiety from the first night of their marriage. After being prepared for bed by her ladies-in-waiting, she relates:

> I remained alone more than two hours not knowing what I ought to do. Should I get up again? Should I stay in bed? I knew nothing. At last my waiting woman, Madame Kruse, came in and reported with great merriment that the Grand Duke [Peter] was waiting on his supper which was about to be brought to him. After His Imperial Highness had supped well, he came to bed, and when he had lain down he began to talk about how it would amuse his servant to see us both in bed. He then fell asleep. . . . The next

morning Madame Kruse tried to question the young married couple. But her hopes proved deceptive. In this state matters remained during the following nine years without alteration.

Peter further impeded their chances for happiness by revealing to his wife, three weeks after their marriage, that he much preferred a certain "Fräulein Carr," a lady of the household. He also boasted of other mistresses, although Catherine never doubted that these "affairs" were merely platonic. In the hopes that Peter would ultimately be able to overcome his impotence, she tried to build a close relationship with him — but to no avail. They would read to each other, but whereas she increasingly turned to serious books on philosophy and politics he cared only for juvenile tales about bandits. Moreover, he devoted much of his time to military exercises. He even insisted on giving Catherine a military polish. "Thanks to his pains," she recalled, "I can shoulder arms to-day as well as the best-drilled grenadier. For hours at a time I had to stand guard with a musket on my shoulders at the door of the room which lay between his room and mine."

When Peter was not drilling his wife, he amused himself by drinking to excess or playing with toy soldiers. He would don the uniform of a general officer and hold elaborate state reviews of his miniature army. One day Catherine came upon him while he was inspecting his troops, and the sight literally paralyzed her with astonishment. In the middle of the room a large rat was suspended from the ceiling. When she asked Peter the meaning of the grotesque spectacle, he replied in all seriousness that the rat had committed the crime of devouring two of his wax soldiers. He had

In 1741 the venal and capricious Anne was succeeded by Peter the Great's daughter Elizabeth, an equally self-indulgent and talentless woman. Eighteen years after her coronation in the Cathedral of the Assumption (near left), Elizabeth's troops seized the Prussian redoubt of Kunersdorf; that major victory in the Seven Years' War is commemorated on the enameled snuffbox at far left. The childless empress did take one issue seriously: she was vitally concerned about the royal succession, and to that end she personally selected both her successor and his bride. Upon Elizabeth's death in 1762 the crown passed to her nephew Peter, who was by that time already married to the future Catherine the Great. The rare silver and niello snuffbox at right bears her likeness.

therefore brought the offender before a military court, which had sentenced the rodent to be hanged.

Despite her growing unhappiness, Catherine never complained. She made many friends at court and always managed to conceal her participation in political intrigue under a cloak of innocence and total submission to her husband and the empress. During those dark days, ambition alone sustained her. She later wrote, "I had at the bottom of my heart I know not what that prevented me from doubting even a moment that sooner or later I should become empress of Russia in my own right."

About this same time Catherine entered into the first of a long series of love affairs. There is evidence to suggest that this initial illicit relationship was arranged by some ladies at the court who knew that Empress Elizabeth was eager for Peter to have an heir — and who apparently realized that Peter was not a likely candidate for fatherhood. Whatever the circumstances, Catherine did have an affair in the early 1750's with the court chamberlain, Sergei Saltykov, whose only distinctions were his good looks and a weakness for the fair sex. In 1754 Catherine gave birth to a son, Paul, and while historians still debate the question of his paternity, it seems unlikely that Peter could have sired the child. In any case, it is beyond dispute that Saltykov made Catherine fully conscious of her sensual needs and powers. After the affair with him ended in 1754, she was rarely without a lover.

Her situation was far from enviable, however. She had become estranged from both Peter and Elizabeth, who had the audacity to remove Catherine's infant son from her care in order to provide him with the special training appropriate for a future monarch. Not until late 1762, when Elizabeth suddenly died, did the wheel of fortune finally turn in Catherine's favor. Peter III succeeded to the throne, but his conduct and policies offended so many people that few Russians in positions of influence expected him to remain in power for long.

Actually, some of Peter's actions were favorably received, especially by the privileged classes. He freed the nobles from obligatory service to the state, abolished the security police, discouraged the arrest of political dissidents, and ordered more lenient treatment of the Old Believers. But at the same time he did much to alienate important groups within the nobility by substantially reducing the authority of the senate, whose members had exercised a considerable amount of power ever since the time of Peter the Great. In addition, his obsession with things German shocked the members of his court. Because he revered Frederick the Great of Prussia, Peter abruptly extricated his country from the war it had been waging against the German state—on terms disadvantageous to Russia. To everyone's amazement, he frequently appeared in public dressed in a Prussian uniform, and once, during a formal state banquet, he interrupted the proceedings by rising from his seat and "prostrating himself headlong" before the bust of Frederick. As if this were not enough, Peter forced rigid Prussian drill exercises upon his nobles and gave precedence to the "Holstein Guards" — soldiers imported from Germany — over the Russian guards. Time and again he referred to Russia as "an accursed land."

His private behavior did not create a better impression. Hardly a day went by that he remained sober un-

til bedtime. Claiming to be an accomplished actor, he would entertain guests at his palace by contorting his face in various ways. On seeing one of the tsar's performances, a lady at court exclaimed that "whatever else he looked like as he was making . . . [the facial expressions], he did not look like a tsar." Andrei Bolotov, a memoirist of the period, accurately summed up the feelings of the people: "The Russians were gnashing their teeth with rage."

Perhaps the most startling feature of Peter's brief reign was his political ineptitude. Not only did he antagonize one social group after another, but his frequent humiliations of Catherine presented the growing opposition with a natural leader around whom it could rally. Thus, for example, he let it be known that he intended to divorce and banish his wife and declare his son, Paul, a bastard. Then at a royal banquet on June 9, 1762, the tsar proposed a toast to the imperial family, making it clear that he had in mind the German as well as the Russian branches of the family. Asserting that the imperial family consisted only of Peter, herself, and their son, Catherine refused to rise from her seat — whereupon the tsar instructed one of his aides-de-camp to denounce the tsarina with a "foul epithet." To make sure that everyone realized that he had insulted his wife, Peter then shouted the obscenity across the table. After this episode, Catherine no longer harbored any compunction about collaborating with those who were planning a coup d'état.

By 1762 the mood of hostility was so pervasive that the most preposterous rumors about Peter were given credence. For example, it was widely believed that he intended to force all the ladies at court to divorce their husbands and marry men of his choosing. He himself was to take the first step by divorcing Catherine and marrying Elizabeth Vorontsovna, who had for some time been his constant companion. But before Peter could undertake any action at all he was deposed — and with such incredible ease that his idol, Frederick of Prussia, was moved to quip that the tsar had "allowed himself to be overthrown as a child is sent to bed."

On July 9, 1762, while Peter was drilling his Holstein Guards, Catherine led thousands of soldiers and nobles into the Church of Our Lady of Kazan — where the royal couple had been married seventeen years earlier — to be formally proclaimed Empress of Russia by the Archbishop of Novgorod. Three days later she could be found "mounted on a white horse, riding at the head of her troops. She wore a uniform, a man's uniform, borrowed from a young lieutenant. Her hat was wreathed with oak-leaves." The empress's destination was Peterhof, the imperial palace, which she seized without resistance. Peter sensed the hopelessness of his situation and quietly abdicated. He ended his erratic and perverse reign of six months incarcerated in a chateau in Ropsha, a few miles from St. Petersburg.

Utterly demoralized, Peter sent Catherine three pathetic letters in which he pleaded with her to be magnanimous. Before the empress could respond to his request, Peter died. According to one report, he was killed on July 16 in a "drunken scuffle after supper." The government announced that he had "expired suddenly of 'colic,'" but few historians doubt that he was murdered. Whether or not Catherine played any role in the deed is an open question. Horace Walpole, son of England's famous prime minister, was convinced —

as were many other contemporary historians — that the empress had instigated the murder even if she herself had not actually committed it. In fact, Walpole referred to her afterward as "Catherine Slay-Czar."

Although resentful of these charges, the empress was not deterred by them. In September 1762, she had herself formally crowned in the Cathedral of the Assumption at the Kremlin. Most knowledgeable people in Europe, aware that she had no legal right to the throne, doubted that she would be able to retain power. But Catherine had other ideas: she quickly crushed several conspiracies, and in so doing demonstrated her determination to rule with an iron hand.

In the public mind Catherine's long reign — from 1762 to 1796 — has gained notoriety because of her phenomenal love life. Indeed, her amorous adventures were unquestionably remarkable, but it would be a mistake to dismiss her as a sovereign who accorded prime interest to private pleasure. Nor would it be accurate to regard her as a self-centered woman who merely used men to satisfy her carnal needs. To be sure, from 1752 until her death she had no fewer than twenty-one lovers, generally men in the prime of life with impressive physiques. It is also true that the older she grew, the younger were the men she chose. When she was in her early sixties, for example, she took a twenty-two-year-old lover. She was passionately devoted to each of her amours at the time of their liaison, and she retained a certain affection for them all afterward. "God is my judge," she stated in 1774, "that I did not take them out of looseness, to which I have no inclination. If fate had given me in youth a husband whom I could have loved, I should have remained al-

ways true to him. The trouble is that my heart would not willingly remain one hour without love."

Several of Catherine's lovers exercised substantial political influence — she even helped Stanislaw Poniatowski acquire the Polish throne after their affair ended — and all were handsomely rewarded by the empress. One, Gregory Potëmkin, allegedly received the stupendous sum of 50,000,000 rubles out of a total of some 92,000,000 that she lavished on her lovers.

Yet despite her time-consuming preoccupation with sensual pleasure, Catherine was a dedicated and hardworking sovereign. Not since Peter the Great had Russia been governed by a ruler as energetic, devoted, and successful as she. She wielded decisive power in formulating and executing state policies in both domestic and foreign affairs.

The most striking aspect of her rule was the sharp contrast between promise and fulfillment, between noble principles and sordid action. For instance, in the late 1760's the empress proclaimed that "Peace is essential to this vast empire; what we need is a larger population, not devastation. . . . Peace will bring us a greater esteem than the always ruinous uncertainties of war." But the exigencies of events and her longing for glory prompted her to undertake several aggressive moves. In 1763, for example, she ordered her troops to seize the duchy of Courland, which was subsequently incorporated into the empire. Thrice she was instrumental in promoting the partition of Poland, and each time she annexed a portion of that unhappy country. Her most significant gains were made at the expense of Turkey, from which she acquired the city of Azov as well as stretches of land along the shores of the Black

Sea in 1774. Nine years later Catherine's troops entered the Crimea, which had been under Turkish rule before 1774, and brought it under the permanent control of the Russian government.

Catherine did not succeed in destroying the Ottoman Empire as she had hoped, but she certainly weakened it substantially. At the same time, her policies were responsible for increasing the size of Russia by 200,000 square miles. The population rose from nineteen to thirty-six million, largely as a result of territorial aggrandizement. These successes in foreign policy, more than any other accomplishments, earned Catherine the title of "Great."

The discrepancy between the empress's avowed goals and her actions was just as pronounced in the domestic realm. She claimed to favor a constitutional form of government based on "European principles," and demonstrated her devotion to liberalism by corresponding regularly with Voltaire and other spokesmen of the French Enlightenment. She genuinely admired their writings and honestly believed herself to be their disciple, but she also knew that contact with the *philosophes* would fashion her reputation as a benevolent and thoughtful ruler. When she heard that Denis Diderot, editor of the massive *Encyclopédie,* was having financial difficulties, she paid him 15,000 francs for his library (which remained in Paris during his lifetime) and appointed him its librarian at an annual salary of 1,000 francs. Moreover, when the French government prohibited the publication of the *Encyclopédie* because of the liberal views found in many of its articles, the empress offered to have it printed in Riga.

In her eagerness to impress the *philosophes,* Cath-

erine on occasion lapsed into unrealistic descriptions of conditions in Russia. She told Voltaire that because she imposed such low taxes on her people "there was not a single peasant in Russia who could not eat chicken whenever he pleased, although he had recently preferred turkey to chicken." She also assured him that "There are no shortages of any kind; people spend their time in singing thanksgiving masses, dancing, and rejoicing."

Not all of Catherine's writings were devoted to self-glorification. In a serious vein she wrote extensively on social, pedagogical, and historical subjects; composed tragedies inspired by Shakespeare's; and wrote librettos for musical comedies. Her *Notes on Russian History,* dealing with the period from the ninth to the thirteenth centuries, is a massive, six-volume work in which she tried to show that Russia's development compared favorably to that of Western countries and that monarchical absolutism had made positive contributions to it. Despite weaknesses in spelling and grammar, and despite her lack of originality, Catherine's discourses impressed the *philosophes* as the products of a thinking person and therefore a kindred soul.

They were flattered beyond words by the attentions showered upon them by the gifted and powerful monarch. Even though Diderot visited Russia in 1773 — and thus had an opportunity to check on some of the empress's claims about conditions in her country — neither he nor most of his colleagues ever challenged her. On the contrary, Diderot heaped praise on her and described her as combining "the soul of Brutus with the charms of Cleopatra." Voltaire exclaimed, "Long live the adorable Catherine," and once, in a burst of

enthusiasm, compared her to Saint Catherine — a title she had the modesty and good sense to reject.

Even a cursory examination of Catherine's domestic policies exposes her liberalism and humanitarianism as shallow, if not downright hypocritical. With much fanfare she convoked a legislative commission in 1767 for the purpose of drawing up a new code of laws based on the most advanced legal doctrines. To guide the commission she drafted a voluminous *Instruction,* composed of 653 sections, in which she expressed her views on every conceivable subject. Although she leaned heavily on the writings of Montesquieu and Beccaria, two well-known liberals on legal questions, her social program turned out to be rather conservative. She was not prepared to reduce the privileges of the nobility and although she suggested an improvement in the lot of the peasants, she did not advocate the abolition of serfdom, Russia's most glaring evil. In any case, the legislative commission was so large and its procedures so cumbersome that it accomplished very little. It did not manage to compile a new code, but it did provide the government with information leading to the administrative reforms enacted after 1775. In a 1785 decree known as the Charter of the Nobility, the empress actually expanded the privileges of the nobles without limiting their tyrannical power over the serfs.

The realization that Catherine merely paid lip service to liberalism emerges with special force from her reaction to Pugachev's rebellion, one of the bloodiest and most threatening peasant uprisings in Russian history. Emelyan Pugachev, an unruly Don Cossack who spent several years in the imperial army and fought in a number of campaigns in Poland and Turkey, was eventually imprisoned for violating military discipline. After escaping, he settled in the territory of the Iaik Cossacks, an area east of the Volga River, and began to stir up disaffected elements of the population against the government. In 1773 he proclaimed himself to be Tsar Peter III, Catherine's husband. He then proceeded to assemble a following of some 30,000 men, whom he organized into a fierce though ragged army. His announced aims were simple: the extermination of government officials and landlords, freedom for the serfs, and the elimination of taxes and military service. In the name of these goals, Pugachev and his irregular troops ravaged the countryside, instituting a veritable reign of terror. Anyone who opposed him risked being murdered by his merciless followers.

When Catherine first learned of the uprising, she was shaken. But she refused to act against the insurgents. In fact, she suppressed all news of the disorders because she feared that rumors of civil unrest would sully her reputation as an enlightened ruler who governed a happy nation. What would Voltaire and Diderot think if they heard about Pugachev? But in July 1774, the pretender stormed the important city of Kazan, and although he did not capture it he did burn much of the town to the ground. At this point Pugachev held a substantial amount of territory in eastern Russia, and it seemed likely that he might attack Moscow itself. Catherine could no longer ignore him. She amassed a large army — against which the rebel's ill-disciplined marauders were no match — and in the fall of 1774 they crushed the insurgents, captured Pugachev, and hauled him to Moscow in a cage. The empress's

Catherine the Great's lengthy flirtation with the French philosophes and her determination to govern her backward nation according to "European principles" both terminated abruptly in 1773. In that year a restive Don Cossack named Emelyan Pugachev declared himself to be Catherine's deceased husband, Peter, rallied a 30,000-man army, and rose against the aristocracy. In 1774 Pugachev was captured, caged (left), and brought to the Kremlin to be tried and executed. Subsequently, Catherine's domestic and foreign policies grew blatantly self-serving, culminating in the empress's attempt to partition European Turkey. With Potëmkin's help, Catherine did manage to annex the Crimea, but she never achieved her dream (below) of adding both Constantinople and Warsaw to her empire.

CONSTANTINOPLE

WARSAW

QUEEN CATHERINES DREAM,

London Pub by W Holland No 50 Oxford St November 4 1791

ministers urged her to make an example of the power-hungry Cossack by subjecting him to various tortures, but she was too conscious of her professed principles for that. Instead, she ordered that he be tried in the Palace of the Kremlin. He was found guilty and executed on January 11, 1775. His head was then strung on a pole, and sections of his dismembered body were put on public exhibition before being burned.

Only a few other rebel leaders were executed. The government preferred to have most of them branded, their nostrils slit, and then sentenced to hard labor. The reprisals carried out against the rebellious peasants were the cruelest aspect of Catherine's policy. The army treated them so savagely that its program of pacification proved as costly in human lives as the uprising itself. All told, the insurrection claimed the lives of 20,000 insurgents and 3,000 officials and nobles. "The Pugachev rebellion," one historian has accurately noted, "served to point out again, forcefully and tragically, the chasm between French philosophy and Russian reality."

From this time on, Catherine the Great grew ever more wary of liberalism, although she tried to conceal her true feelings under a barrage of lofty pronouncements. But when she learned of the progress of the French Revolution — which had been inspired by some of the ideas she had formerly embraced — she could no longer remain silent. "One never knows," she wrote in January 1791, "if you are living in the midst of the murders, carnage, and uproar of the den of thieves who have seized upon the government of France, and will soon turn it into Gaul as it was in the time of Caesar. But Caesar put them down! When will this Caesar come! Oh, come he will, you need not doubt." The execution of Louis XVI two years later drove her into a paroxysm of fury: "The very name of France should be exterminated! Equality is a monster. It would fain be king!"

Within Russia itself, Catherine refused to tolerate any ideas that displeased her. In 1790, for example, Alexander Radishchev, a sensitive and courageous man, created something of a sensation by publishing his *Journey from Petersburg to Moscow,* an exposé of the horrors of serfdom, despotism, and administrative corruption. The empress acknowledged that Radishchev was a man of "imagination" and "learning," but she could not forgive him for revealing that evils existed in Russia. "The purpose of this book," she declared, "is clear on every page: its author, infected by and full of the French madness, is trying in every possible way to break down respect for authority . . . to stir up in the people indignation against their superiors and against the government." Radishchev was arrested, tried for fomenting sedition, and sentenced to death. This barbaric penalty was commuted, probably on Catherine's recommendation, to ten years' exile in Siberia.

The divergence between word and deed that marked Catherine's political and social programs also characterized her promotion of artistic endeavors. Thus, she decided to rebuild the Kremlin primarily because an undertaking of that order would enhance her reputation. She herself was not particularly fond of the ancient citadel: on her first visit there — for her betrothal to Peter in 1744 — she complained of its dark and drafty residences. Nevertheless, the Kremlin remained the major architectural landmark in Russia — and not

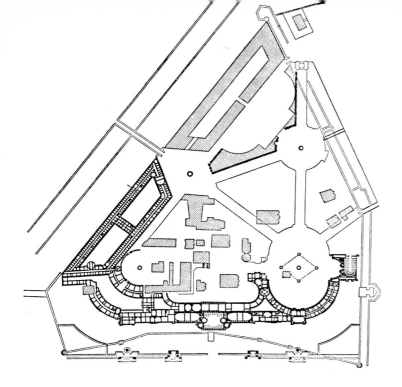

since the late 1740's, when Rastrelli had built a small baroque palace facing the Moscow River for Empress Elizabeth, had any noteworthy structure been erected in the former capital. Moreover, Catherine had learned that Westerners thought the Russian government bankrupt — and by publicly committing twenty to thirty million rubles to a grand architectural enterprise, she intended to convince the world that the story was groundless. She also wanted more resplendent quarters for her own occasional visits to Moscow: indeed, she desired nothing less than an "Eastern Versailles." The new Kremlin would be an eternal monument to the greatness of her reign.

Catherine assigned this awesome task to a brilliant young native architect, Vasili Bazhenov, who had suggested the idea of a thoroughly renovated Kremlin to the empress on an earlier occasion. As the son of a humble clergyman, Bazhenov had originally attended the Slavonic-Greek Latin Academy in Moscow to prepare himself for the priesthood, but from the first he displayed such outstanding talent for drawing that his father eventually enrolled him in Prince Ukhtomski's school of architecture. In 1760 Bazhenov went to Paris to continue his studies under the renowned Charles de Wailly. At the French Academy he performed so superbly that had he not been a foreigner he would have won the coveted Prix de Rome. He completed his European tour by working at the Roman and Florentine academies for three years. By the time he returned to St. Petersburg in 1765 the twenty-eight-year-old artist had already earned an international reputation.

Motivated by jealousy of the newcomer, the archi-

tects in the Russian capital — both French and Italian — did their utmost to prevent him from obtaining royal commissions. For a time he was obliged to work for the artillery services in Moscow. But Bazhenov's dazzling reputation could not be hidden from the sovereign. In 1768–69 she had him design a new arsenal in St. Petersburg. The structure was his first major undertaking, one clearly "impregnated with French taste." Soon thereafter Catherine accepted his offer to reconstruct the Kremlin.

Bazhenov devoted months to making drawings and constructing a large wooden model of his proposed design. He planned to preserve the oldest and most important dynastic shrines, but many others were slated for demolition. The remaining buildings would be enclosed by a gigantic, triangular four-story palace, which, according to one authority, "was to contain a series of sumptuous formal salons, living quarters for the empress and her suite, a church, a theater, picture galleries, a library, service quarters, and all the necessary appurtenances for royal pomp and luxury." The principal feature of this palace — its columns and colonnades — would make it a "hymn to the column," according to its architect. From the wooden model it is evident that its designer borrowed heavily from the huge French royal chateaux and Renaissance palaces of eighteenth-century Europe.

In 1769 Bazhenov began to implement his plans. A few of the ancient buildings and towers scheduled for destruction were razed, and on June 1, 1773, Catherine attended a glittering formal ceremony at the Kremlin to celebrate the laying of the cornerstone for the palace. Unfortunately for Bazhenov — but fortunately

Two years after the cornerstone of the new Kremlin was laid, Catherine precipitously abandoned the entire project. Russia's triumph over the Turks in 1774 had restored the nation's international prestige, and Catherine no longer needed the mammoth renovation project to bolster her country's sagging reputation. In 1776 Catherine did add the triangular Senate Building (below) to the northeast corner of the Kremlin compound, but by that time it was evident that her interest in the ancient citadel had waned.

for posterity — Catherine soon lost interest in the project. Her change of mind resulted from the increase in prestige she had gained with the conclusion of the Turkish war in 1774. Having reaped a considerable amount of favorable publicity from the grand enterprise, she shrewdly calculated that she did not need to spend so much money refurbishing the Kremlin. In 1775, once the Western world knew that she nurtured great ambitions, she halted Bazhenov's work.

Despite her change of heart, the empress did not altogether neglect the Kremlin. She invited Matvei Kazakov, who had served as an assistant to Bazhenov, to design the Archbishop's House, which was built in the 1770's. Kazakov also drafted plans for the Senate Building (erected between 1776 and 1787), in which the offices of the Supreme Soviet of the USSR have been located since 1918. Thus despite the fact that Catherine's contributions to the Kremlin did not live up to her original lofty pronouncements, they were by no means inconsequential.

By the empress's lights, her reign surely amounted to a success. Her most intense ambitions — to be popular in literate circles and to gain a reputation for having enhanced the glory and power of Russia — were realized. Yet in the closing years of her life she was tormented by the thought that the throne would pass to her unstable son, Paul, with whom she had never gotten along. Since Paul assumed Peter III had been his father, he understandably believed himself entitled to rule instead of his mother. In part because she was aware that many Russians believed his claim to be legitimate, Catherine had always kept Paul at bay and even allowed several of her favorites to humiliate him.

Moreover, her announced intention to disinherit him could only contribute to his hostility toward her and his anger over the weakness of his position. For some unknown reason, Catherine failed to designate her beloved grandson Alexander as her successor — and as a result, when she died in 1796 the royal court once again became the center of countless intrigues. Five years after her demise the last of Russia's palace coups occurred: Paul was assassinated by conspirators and succeeded by Alexander, who was destined to rule during one of the most trying times in the country's modern history: the Napoleonic invasion.

VII
Russia under the Romanovs

No politically sophisticated contemporary of Tsar Alexander I would have dared to predict his victory over the redoubtable Napoleon, Emperor of France and dictator of much of the European continent. Alexander, who was subject to diverse and contradictory influences, appeared too weak and vacillating to stand up to the French ruler. A professed liberal who often followed reactionary policies, Alexander claimed to cherish peace yet showed himself to be a "drill sergeant and parade ground enthusiast" whose expansionist dreams were realized at the expense of Persia, Turkey, and Sweden. Although reputed to be a clever and rational diplomat, the tsar had become so imbued with mysticism by 1812 that it adversely affected his political conduct. Because of these and other contradictions in his character, historians have referred to Alexander as the "sphinx," the "enigmatic tsar," and the "crowned Hamlet."

Personal considerations aside, Alexander suffered such tribulations at the hands of Napoleon during the first decade of the nineteenth century that even today it seems inconceivable that he should have triumphed over the outstanding military genius of the age. From 1805 to 1807 the tsar had joined forces with Austria and Prussia to halt the emperor's advance into Western and Central Europe, but in that two-year period Russia was dealt three crushing blows – at Austerlitz, Jena, and Friedland. When Napoleon offered peace, the tsar readily agreed to negotiate. In July 1807, the two sovereigns met on a gaily decorated raft in the middle of the Nieman River, near the town of Tilsit, and reached an agreement that in effect permitted France to dominate Western Europe and Russia to dominate

Eastern Europe. The arrangement suited Napoleon – at least for the time being – because it allowed him to concentrate on the struggle with Great Britain, the one major country he had been unable to defeat.

Over the next few years Alexander fawned on Napoleon, but the Franco-Russian alliance was foredoomed despite his efforts. The Russian nobles implored the tsar to break relations with France, fearing that "the child of the Revolution," as the emperor was known, would export liberal ideas that might ultimately infect Russia. Then suddenly, in one area after another, the interests of the two nations collided. The single most important source of friction was Russia's unwillingness to honor the Continental System, the economic blockade that Napoleon had mounted against Great Britain. The system was so detrimental to Russian exporters and landlords that they persistently disregarded it, but Napoleon was not the kind of man to stand idly by and witness the subversion of his plans.

There are also indications that the emperor was affected by fits of megalomania during this period. "Now we shall march on Moscow," he declared in 1812, "and from Moscow why not turn to India? Let no one tell Napoleon that it is far from Moscow to India! . . . Just suppose . . . that Moscow is taken, that Russia lies prostrate, . . . will it be impossible for the French army to reach the Ganges with the help of auxiliary forces? And once the French sword touches the Ganges, the edifice of England's mercantile greatness will tumble in ruins." This bravado stemmed from Napoleon's unshakable faith in his own invincibility. After his stunning victory at Friedland in 1807 he had told his brother: "I can do everything now."

On June 24, 1812, without bothering to declare war, Napoleon led his Grand Army across the Nieman River into Russian territory — thus beginning the most momentous struggle of his career. In a desperate effort to avoid hostilities, Alexander pleaded with his adversary to withdraw, but the invader could not be deterred. The emperor had mustered an enormous force of some 600,000 men for the campaign, and although he seems to have lacked a precise plan, he did press forward. If Napoleon ascribed the tsar's plea to personal weakness, he was soon to be disillusioned, for it turned out that in the face of severe provocation Alexander could summon up a tenacity and courage that startled his subjects as well as his foes. As one of his ministers aptly remarked: "Alexander is too weak to rule and too strong to be ruled."

For more than a century and a half it has been generally believed that the Russian generals followed a "Scythian strategy" in response to the invasion — that is, they deliberately lured the enemy into a devastated country knowing that its citizens would refuse to give the invaders much-needed provisions. In support of this thesis historians cite, among other things, a statement by Alexander to General Armand de Caulaincourt, one of Napoleon's intimates: "Your Frenchman is brave; but long privations and a bad climate wear him down and discourage him. Our climate, our winter, will fight on our side. With you, marvels take place where the emperor is in personal attendance; and he cannot be everywhere, he cannot be absent from Paris year after year." These comments notwithstanding, no strategy of retreat was ever devised by the Russian high command.

In truth, the Russian army retreated because the generals correctly judged their forces to be too weak to stop the French. At most the defenders could deploy 150,000 men, which meant that they were outnumbered four to one. An additional weakness of the Russian Army, according to the most recent authority on the subject, was the "ignorance and military incompetence of many officers, even generals." Furthermore, demoralization had set in because of widespread corruption among the officers and the barbaric discipline imposed on common soldiers. "Much use was made of the bastinado [cudgel]. The principle was: beat two to death, train the third." Rank-and-file soldiers found this brutal treatment so unbearable that they often committed suicide to escape it.

In view of these handicaps, General Barclay de Tolly, who made most of the major decisions during the first part of the campaign, had little choice but to pull back. But in so doing he prevented Napoleon from achieving his prime objective in every previous war — the early destruction of the opposing force. With each successive day the emperor occupied more territory, but he could not claim victory. Nor could he relax for a single moment: the enemy might suddenly decide to fight.

About six weeks after the campaign was launched several of Napoleon's marshals warned him that he was falling into a trap. They pointed out that the Grand Army was already beginning to feel the strain of the long march: in the advance from Vilna to Vitebsk, for example, 8,000 of the army's 22,000 horses had died. In addition, the retreating Russians had devastated much of the countryside. As a result Napoleon's forces could not live off the conquered lands, as

was their custom, and transporting supplies all the way from Poland presented tremendous logistical problems. But the most ominous sign for the French was that despite his territorial losses Alexander refused to sue for peace. Nonetheless, Napoleon continued the chase. "If necessary," he told one of his advisers, "I shall go as far as Moscow, the holy city of Moscow, in quest of battle, and I shall win the battle." At that point Alexander would be forced to capitulate — "for a capital to be occupied by an enemy is equivalent to a girl losing her honor."

In the meantime, the Russian public unleashed a barrage of criticism at the generals for their failure to fight. Late in August the tsar yielded to the pressure of his counselors and appointed sixty-seven-year-old Prince Michael Kutuzov commander in chief — even though the sovereign passionately disliked him. Kutuzov was a highly respected officer, and in the hope of restoring national unity and bolstering morale in the army, Alexander set aside his personal feelings. One of the few who looked upon retreat as the most viable strategy, Kutuzov promptly announced that he intended to give up the ancient citadel and former capital without a struggle. But according to General Karl von Clausewitz, the noted German strategist who accompanied the Russian army, "the court, the army, and the whole of Russia" clamored for battle. For essentially political reasons, therefore, Kutuzov decided to make a stand in defense of Moscow.

On September 7 a Russian force of 112,000 met a French army of 130,000 near Borodino, about seventy-five miles southwest of the ancient city. Although the fighting lasted only one day, the blood-letting was savage. The Russians lost 58,000 men and the French 50,000, including forty-seven of their best generals. The outcome can only be described as uncertain, for while the Russians withdrew again, their morale was high and their retreat orderly. The battle of Borodino was at least a great moral triumph for Russia. After Napoleon had been deposed, he himself acknowledged its significance: "The most terrible of all my battles was the one before Moscow. The French showed themselves worthy of victory, and the Russians worthy of being invincible."

Several generals urged Kutuzov to engage the French again before Moscow, but the commander insisted on withdrawal. "You fear a retreat through Moscow," he told a conference of his highest officers, "but I regard it as far-sighted, because it will save the army. Napoleon is like a stormy torrent which we are as yet unable to stop. Moscow will be the sponge that will suck him in." So thoroughly did this decision depress Kutuzov that when he entered his private quarters he broke into uncontrollable weeping — but he would not change his mind.

Triumphantly, Napoleon marched toward Moscow, and on the morning of September 14, 1812, he reached the Sparrow Hills, which overlook the city. He ordered Joachim I Napoleon, the King of Naples, to bring a "deputation of city authorities" to meet him at Moscow's principal gate. They were supposed to surrender the keys, as had been the custom in every other major town he had occupied. To the emperor's astonishment, Joachim returned a short time later to report that he "had not discovered so much as a single prominent inhabitant." Indeed, it soon became apparent that out of a population of 250,000 only about 12,000 citizens remained. "Moscow is empty!" the emperor cried in disbelief. "Incredible! We must enter. Go and bring some of the boyars." Stubbornly, he continued to wait for a few hours on the Sparrow Hills. "Finally, an officer, either anxious to please or convinced that everything desired by the emperor must take place, penetrated the city, caught five or six vagrants, and, pushing them forward with his horse, brought them into the presence of the emperor, imagining that he had brought a deputation." This action only compounded the injury to the ruler's pride, for "from the very answers of these unfortunates, Napoleon saw that he had before him but a few pitiful day-laborers."

Toward evening Napoleon finally entered the city, not in the mood of exhilaration he had anticipated but in one of gloom. Early the next morning he rode to the Kremlin — and the sight of the fortress raised his spirits. "The city is as big as Paris," he wrote to his wife. "There are 1,600 church towers here, and over a thousand beautiful palaces; the city is provided with everything." He occupied the royal palace that Rastrelli had built for Empress Elizabeth, and settled in for some much-needed rest. But before he could obtain even one night's sleep, the emperor was obliged to flee for his life.

At eight o'clock in the evening of September 15 a fire — presumably touched off by the careless French soldiers who were looting the capital — erupted in one of the suburbs. Orders were given to extinguish it and the imperial party retired for the night. Two and a half hours later Caulaincourt was awakened by his valet, who told him that flames were spreading over a large part of the city. "I had only to open my eyes," Caulaincourt recalled, "to realize that this was so, for the fire was giving off so much light it was bright enough to read in the middle of the night." A strong wind from the north drove the flames toward the center; the wooden houses burned like tinderboxes.

Additional fires broke out in other districts, and by four o'clock in the morning the conflagration had enveloped so much of the city that the emperor had to be roused from his sleep. Within a few hours the Kremlin itself was threatened. "The air was so hot, and the pine-wood sparks were so numerous that the beams supporting the iron plates which formed the roof of the Arsenal all caught fire," Caulaincourt remembered. "The roof of the Kremlin kitchen was only saved by men being placed there with brooms and buckets to gather up the glowing fragments and moisten the beams. Only by superhuman efforts was the fire in the Arsenal extinguished. The emperor was there himself; his presence inspired the Guard to every exertion."

It soon became too dangerous for Napoleon to remain in the Kremlin, and accompanied by his closest advisers and personal guards he managed to escape. He set up headquarters in a country mansion just outside Moscow. The metropolis continued to burn for another two days, and when the flames at last subsided about 90 per cent of the city had been destroyed. Most of the structures in the Kremlin remained intact, however — and fortunately for the French, the grain and fodder warehouses along the wharves also escaped, leaving the army with provisions for six months.

The burning of Moscow stunned and disheartened

To compound Napoleon's miseries, the winter of
1812 proved to be one of the severest in memory,
and the bitter winds that swept the steppes
threatened to cut the emperor's precarious lifeline
to the West. A mere five weeks after his entry into
Moscow, Napoleon was obliged to relinquish his
prize. A contemporary cartoon (left), published in
London in December 1812, shows "General Frost"
shaving "Little Boney." The Kremlin burns in the
background, perhaps as a result of the dynamite
charges planted by the retreating French. As the
Grand Army attempted to ford the Berezina River,
the wily Russians struck in full force. An eyewitness
watercolor (right) of that chaotic scene gives ample
evidence of the sort of hardships that reduced the
massive French invasion force from 600,000 to
30,000 men in less than five months.

Napoleon, who now referred to the Russians as "Scyth-
ians" and "barbarians." He could not control his anger:
"This exceeds all imagination. This is a war of extermination. Such terrible tactics have no precedent in the
history of civilization. . . . To burn one's own cities!
. . . A demon inspires these people! What savage determination! What a people! What a people!" Napoleon's
professions of outrage might have sounded more con-
vincing had he himself observed the canons of civilized
behavior when he returned to the Kremlin on September 18. Among his more outrageous acts was the
quartering of cavalry mounts in the Uspenski sobor
and the removal from it of more than five tons of silver
and gold. (Cossack troops eventually recovered most of
this booty and returned it to the church.)

As soon as the fire had burned itself out, the French
authorities conducted an investigation. They concluded that Count Rostopchin, governor-general of
Moscow, had planned the burning and evacuation of
the city. The investigators alleged that all the fire
engines had either been removed or damaged and that
fuses had been found in numerous buildings, including the imperial bedroom in the Kremlin. Finally,
the French claimed to have discovered four hundred
arsonists — whom they summarily tried and executed.

The evidence in support of this explanation is far
from conclusive, and historians are still debating the
question of responsibility. Rostopchin himself did not
help to clarify the issue: initially, when he thought the
burning of Moscow would be popular, he took credit
for it; later, when he realized that the people deplored
the action, he denied any connection with it. Of course
it served the interests of the French to place the blame

on the Russians, if only to forestall being blamed for
it themselves. For if the Russians came to believe that
Napoleon had intentionally devastated their holy city,
they would detest the invader with even greater intensity than before. Despite the emperor's elaborate investigations, this is precisely what happened. In truth, it
is quite likely that no one deliberately set the fires, and
that, as Leo Tolstoi argues in War and Peace, they
broke out accidentally. Because the city was empty, no
one extinguished them — and the winds took over.

After Moscow was razed, Napoleon's occupation of
the city could no longer pressure Alexander into suing
for peace. Quite the contrary: the tsar held the French
responsible for the disaster, and he became more
adamant than ever in his refusal to deal with them. "It
is Napoleon or I, either he or I — we can no longer
reign at the same time! I have found him out and he
will not deceive me again." Melodramatically, Alexander vowed that he would "eat potatoes with the
lowliest of my peasants in the depths of Siberia" rather
than negotiate with the "monster who is the misfortune
of the entire world."

Never before had Napoleon's plans misfired so completely. He had captured the former capital, but he
had not defeated Russia. Moreover, he soon saw that he
could not stay in Moscow for long. Once winter set in
he would find it difficult if not impossible to maintain
contact with the rest of his empire and to secure adequate military supplies. His prolonged absence from
Western Europe might well stimulate open resistance
in conquered lands. Finally, discipline in the Grand
Army — only one third of which was French — began
to decline; numerous soldiers deserted, and many

others showed greater interest in looting than in maintaining French control over Russian territory.

For the first time in his career Napoleon was indecisive. He considered a four-hundred-mile march on St. Petersburg, but gave up that idea when his marshals convinced him that it was too risky, especially since inclement weather might soon hamper the movement of a large army. Out of sheer desperation he made three separate peace overtures to Alexander, but the tsar did not even bother to reply. On October 18 Kutuzov inflicted substantial casualties on the French in a minor skirmish, and a day later — after five weeks in Moscow — Napoleon ordered his army to begin the march back to the West.

So great was Napoleon's anger at Alexander that he spitefully decided to annihilate the Kremlin. For three days Russian citizens were forced to lay mines in palaces, churches, and other structures. As soon as the army had left, the explosions erupted, causing extensive damage to the Arsenal and to portions of the Kremlin wall and several of its towers. A fortuitous rainfall prevented most of the fuses from igniting, but if nature had not intervened, Napoleon's barbaric action would probably have led to the destruction of most of the Kremlin.

Nature was also largely responsible for the destruction of the retreating Grand Army. Short of supplies, ill-equipped to cope with the severe winter that set in earlier than usual, harassed both by Kutuzov's troops and roving guerrillas, the vast military machine rapidly disintegrated. The horses collapsed in droves, mainly because they were improperly shod and could not keep their footing on the ice. "For dozens of miles," we are told, "the roads were littered with corpses. Soldiers built shelters with the corpses of their comrades, piling them like logs." It has been estimated that no more than 30,000 men survived the Russian campaign — one out of twenty. The crushing defeat marked the beginning of the end of Napoleon's grand scheme to subjugate the entire European continent. For Alexander, it marked the beginning of the most glorious phase in his career; during the next few years he was not only one of the most influential but also one of the most popular monarchs in Europe.

Neither the Russian government nor the Russian people wasted much time before beginning to rebuild Moscow. Shortly after Napoleon's departure the inhabitants trekked back into the city, and in 1814 Alexander commissioned the architect Osip Beauvais to supervise the reconstruction of Red Square, the first of Moscow's public plazas to be repaired. Four years later, in a fitting gesture of patriotism, Ivan Martos's monument to Minin and Pozharsky, the liberators of Moscow in 1611, was erected in the square. In the meantime, masons repaired the damaged Kremlin.

After 1825, when nationalism and reaction became the dominant political currents in the country, the government launched a more ambitious building program in the citadel. Unlike his brother Alexander, Tsar Nicholas I, who ruled from 1825 to 1855, subscribed to a consistent and uncomplicated theory of politics summarized in three words: orthodoxy, autocracy, and nationality. Convinced that he ruled by the grace of God, Nicholas envisioned a "state organized and functioning like a well-drilled army unit." At times Nicholas's arbitrariness manifested itself in absurd

actions. Because he disliked the smell of tobacco, for example, he prohibited smoking not only in his palace but in all of St. Petersburg. In signing a document annulling a marriage he wrote in the margin: "The young person shall be considered a virgin."

It was only natural that a sovereign who glorified Russia's national traditions should pay special attention to the ancient capital, Moscow. Nicholas generously sponsored the work of Konstantin Ton, a German-Russian architect who strove to "create a 'genuine' Russian style based on old motifs derived from 'Russian-Byzantine,' 'Russian-Gothic' and even 'Russian-Hindu-Gothic' architecture." His major contribution, the quadrangular Grand Kremlin Palace, took ten years to build (1839 to 1849) and occupies almost 500,000 square feet. To make room for it Ton had to demolish several old structures, but he did incorporate the existing Golden Tsaritsa Chamber, the Palace of Facets, and the Terem Palace into the sprawling edifice. Most architectural experts consider the Grand Kremlin Palace a "sorry successor" to the earlier royal residences of the capital. Ton's attempt to fuse various styles from different eras amounted to little more than superficial imitation of the past.

Yet its massiveness, luxury, and opulence make the palace an impressive sight. "The interiors are decorated with rare wood, malachite pilasters, marble and alabaster columns, crystal chandeliers, and much gold," according to one architectural authority. Its largest room, the Hall of Saint George, is two hundred feet long, sixty-eight feet wide and fifty-eight feet high. Marble slabs inscribed with the names and dates of outstanding regiments adorn the walls. The Alexander

Alexander I's wholly unexpected triumph over the French thrust Russia into the mainstream of European politics after 1812, and Russian architecture of the period reflects that new internationalism. The Grand Kremlin Palace, erected in the 1840's by Alexander's successor, Nicholas I, envelops a half dozen older buildings, both lay and ecclesiastical. Its smaller public rooms (left) are, in general, little more than slavish copies of Western salons, but the three great halls are constructed on a scale that is distinctly Russian. The gleaming Hall of Saint Vladimir (left below) links five centuries of Russian architecture, for its doors give onto the Palace of Facets and the Terem Palace. The latter is a compendium of Russian decorative arts; the royal bedchamber (below), for example, combines the tiled stoves, exuberantly painted walls, and stained glass that epitomize seventeenth-century Russian decor.

Hall, built in honor of the Order of Alexander Nevsky, has pink walls sheathed with imitation marble and embellished with gold. And the Hall of Saint Vladimir, which once served as the throne room of the tsar, "has square columns and vaulted ceilings decorated with flowers of gold and heraldic devices." After 1918 the Bolshevik government combined the latter two halls into one large chamber for the annual meetings of the Supreme Soviet.

In 1839 Ton began work on the Church of the Redeemer in commemoration of the Napoleonic wars of 1812–14. Here again the architect tried to "graft Byzantine detail on a classical form" — once more with only dubious success. In the 1930's this church was razed to make room for the Palace of Congresses, but the sculptures and decorative details have been preserved. Ton's last major work was the Oruzheinaia palata, or Armory, which contains more than ten thousand art treasures ranging from elaborate medieval snuffboxes to the regalia of the tsars. Its holdings also include collections of antique arms, some of them manufactured as early as the sixteenth century in one of the Kremlin's first armories. The Oruzheinaia palata is without doubt the richest repository of historical artifacts in all of Russia.

After Tsar Nicholas's death in 1855 the government continued to promote old Russian architecture, the outstanding example of which is Moscow's Historical Museum, erected between 1874 and 1883 by V. O. Sherwood, an artist of English descent. Situated next to the Kremlin wall opposite the Cathedral of Saint Basil the Blessed, the Historical Museum assaults the eye with its octagonal towers, tent roofs, and superimposed arches piled on top of each other "without any understanding of the contrast of masses which had been the formal principle of old Russian architecture." Nonetheless, it represents one of the more successful latter-day attempts to re-create the spirit of traditional Russian art.

The government's sponsorship of these expensive enterprises would seem to suggest a stable, prosperous, and successful political order. In fact, the opposite was the case. Beginning in the 1850's, the tsarist regime endured numerous failures in foreign policy and increasing domestic unrest. Russia's military forces performed poorly in four wars and suffered decisive defeats in three of them. In large measure these setbacks can be explained by the country's archaic social and political institutions. In 1861 the government issued its own emancipation proclamation abolishing serfdom — which in Russia amounted to virtual slavery — but the lot of the peasants, who constituted the bulk of the population, steadily deteriorated. The prodigious fecundity of peasant families led to a per capita decline in their landholdings. The peasant masses lived so close to the subsistence margin that a single crop failure could mean starvation — and such failures plagued the country in the nineteenth century. The misery of the Russian people is vividly illustrated by the following statistics: early in the twentieth century the death rate per thousand was 31.0, compared with 15.4 in England and Wales.

In 1881 a group of intellectuals, made desperate by the wretchedness of the masses, assassinated Tsar Alexander II. During the next three-and-a-half decades political assassinations occurred with increasing frequency. The acceleration of industrialization in the

1890's exacerbated these social and political tensions. Industrial workers living at close quarters in the cities found it much easier to organize and to pressure the government for reforms than did the peasants. The middle classes also became an organized political force during this period, demanding far-reaching changes that would lead to a new constitutional order. Indeed, by 1905 opposition to the autocracy had grown so vigorous that it almost succeeded in overthrowing the government. Despite months of turbulence and bloodshed the monarchy clung to power, but the disaffection was so intense that only fundamental changes could have prevented further upheavals. Unfortunately, the man at the helm of state was incapable of understanding the gravity of the situation.

Nicholas II, who came to power in 1894, possessed none of the qualities necessary to rule a major power, much less to cope with complex crises. His chief failing was not lack of intelligence but rather startling immaturity. In 1893, for example, the twenty-five-year-old tsarevich noted in his diary that he and two friends "played hide-and-seek just like small children." A year later he and Prince George of Greece fought a battle with chestnuts: "We started in front of the house and ended on the roof."

The reader of Nicholas's diary is likely to be most surprised by the tsar's indifference to affairs of state. He takes pains to describe the activities of his family, the weather, the military reviews and maneuvers he attended, and — above all — his performance in the numerous sports in which he loved to participate. He never fails to mention exactly how many animals he had bagged on a particular shooting expedition. The

reader searches in vain, however, for extensive comments on such momentous political events as the Russo-Japanese War or the Revolution of 1905. Yet despite his apparent preoccupation with domestic trivia, Nicholas fervently believed in the institution of autocracy and staunchly resisted any suggestion that he give up one iota of his power.

His weak character made matters worse, for he readily came under the influence of disreputable or politically irresponsible people. The person who eventually swayed him most was his wife, Alexandra, the former Princess Alix of Hesse-Darmstadt, whom he married in 1894 and with whom he enjoyed a remarkably happy relationship. Even in middle age they expressed a tenderness and affection for each other that one would normally expect only from young lovers. Throughout their marriage Nicholas remained a faithful husband and devoted father, qualities not displayed by many tsars.

Initially, their sole personal distress derived from Alexandra's failure to give birth to a son, although she did have four daughters. Highly mystical in her religious beliefs, the tsarina sought the guidance of "charlatans and adventurers" — and in 1904 she and Nicholas were at last blessed with a son. To the couple's dismay the child, Alexis, suffered from hemophilia, and in their grief the parents turned for help to a self-proclaimed prophet and healer, a semiliterate peasant from Siberia named Gregory Rasputin.

Not much is known about Rasputin's early life beyond the simple fact that he was born in 1872 in the province of Tobolsk, 250 miles east of the Ural mountains. As a young man he gained a reputation for horse stealing and lust, and in the early 1890's he married

All Moscow was illuminated for the coronation of the last Tsar and Autocrat of All the Russias in 1896. Momentarily eschewing their welling antimonarchism, the citizens of Moscow thronged to the glittering Kremlin (center below) for the investiture of Nicholas II and his elegant wife, Alexandra. When the protracted ceremony ended, the new tsar received official blessings from the patriarch of Moscow in a service conducted in the Cathedral of the Assumption (far right). Scenes from the royal family's daily life decorate the gold and enamel "Easter egg" at right, a gift from the doting tsar to his devoted wife on the fifteenth anniversary of the ceremony in 1911.

and sired three children, two girls and one mentally defective boy. Neither marriage nor fatherhood led him to constrain his search for sexual adventures, but his wife apparently did not mind. "He has enough for all," she explained.

At some point — no one knows precisely when — Rasputin underwent a religious experience of sorts. According to some accounts, he joined an illegal mystical sect. He then disappeared from Siberia. For a few years he adopted the life-style of the *stranniki*, ascetic wanderers who traveled throughout the country and lived off charity. After two pilgrimages to Jerusalem, Rasputin showed up at the religious academy in St. Petersburg in December 1903. The monk Illiodor, who met him at the time, remembered him as a "stocky peasant of middle height, with ragged and dirty hair falling over his shoulders, tangled beard, and steely-grey eyes, deep set under their bushy eyebrows, which sometimes almost sank into pin points, and a strong body odor." Illiodor and other clergymen were impressed by Rasputin's declaration that he wished to repent for his sins by serving God, and they helped him get settled in St. Petersburg.

Somehow, the belief spread in high society that Rasputin could perform miracles. His first achievement is said to have been the cure of a dog beloved by the Grand Duke Nicholas, the tsar's uncle. Late in 1905 Rasputin was introduced to the tsar and tsarina, and he immediately captivated the royal couple by stopping young Alexis's bleeding. The tsarina did not doubt that Rasputin "was a holy man, almost a Christ." She also interpreted his appearance at the court as a sign of the mystical union between the peasants and autocracy; a

man of the people had come to save the dynasty.

So many observers have reported the beneficial effects of Rasputin's treatments on the Tsarevich Alexis that it is impossible to ignore them, but there is no reason to ascribe these results to miraculous powers. There seems little question that the bleeding was arrested by means of hypnosis.

During this period Rasputin entered into innumerable affairs, and his partners were often ladies close to the imperial court. "If he stopped before the women to kiss them three times with bowed head," his biographer tells us, "they thrilled with the ecstasy of a religious experience, and called him by names proper only to a saint. They were convinced that God revealed himself in his words, that the Holy Ghost met them in the glance of his little, water-blue eyes, that his touch transmitted even to their sinful bodies the grace dwelling in him, and that his kisses and embraces sanctified each of his faithful disciples." Some men actually felt honored to be cuckolded by the lascivious "monk."

Many people in St. Petersburg were scandalized by Rasputin's conduct, however, and publicly denounced him. In 1912 a lecturer at the religious academy of the Trinity and Saint Sergius attacked the mystic as a heretic and "fornicator of human souls and bodies." Neither these charges nor Rasputin's seduction of the tsarevich's nurse made the slightest impression on Nicholas or his wife. On the contrary, after World War I began in August 1914, Alexandra relied on the man she called "our Friend" more than ever. The full significance of this dependence became evident in 1915 when Nicholas, having assumed the position of commander in chief, spent much of his time at the front and

allowed his wife to play a major role in supervising domestic policies.

Russia, whose bureaucracy proved incapable of coping with the economic and social problems engendered by the war, suffered defeat after defeat — and all the while Alexandra urged her husband to "be more autocratic . . . show your mind." Worse still, she begged him to "hearken to our Friend." In October 1916, with Russia verging on complete collapse, she pleaded with the tsar to leave the front for a while to visit Rasputin.

By this time Rasputin wielded an enormous amount of power; a leading historian maintains that he was "the undisputed master of the destinies of the country." During 1915 and 1916, when the government in its weakness experienced numerous changes, the "Holy Devil," as he was widely known, exerted decisive influence in determining appointments. Early in 1916 Alexandra urged Nicholas to appoint the incompetent Boris Stürmer as chief minister because he "very much values Gregory . . . and completely believes in [his] wonderful, God-sent wisdom." Unfortunately for Russia — and for himself — Nicholas heeded the advice.

This unprecedented situation caused such despair among people well-disposed toward the monarchy that in December 1916, several archconservatives took it upon themselves to assassinate Rasputin. Prince Felix Yusupov, who was married to one of the tsar's nieces, organized the conspiracy and fired the first shots into the Holy Devil. Poisoned wine and cakes had failed to fell Rasputin, and Yusupov's bullets did not finish him either. The conspirators were finally obliged to drown the mystic in the Neva River.

The conspirators expected Rasputin's murder to "be

Although dilatory, obstinate, and ill-informed
in matters of state, Nicholas II was a concerned and
compassionate father. Indeed, it was his unremitting
anxiety over his hemophiliac son, Alexis (seen
at left with his four older sisters), that drew him
into Gregory Rasputin's invidious thrall. Rasputin,
a subliterate, itinerant faith healer, managed to
stem the tsarevich's bleeding through hypnosis —
a feat that earned him the tsarina's boundless
gratitude and gained him entrée to the innermost
councils at court. There his womanizing,
exemplified by this 1917 photograph entitled
"Rasputin at his Court," created a scandal that
undermined the tsar's power and ultimately cost
the "Holy Devil" his life.

On March 8, 1917, an angry but disorganized mob swelled the streets of Petrograd in an apparently spontaneous paroxysm of antimonarchism. That event — known as the February Revolution in Russia, which had not yet converted to the Gregorian calendar — signaled the start of the Russian Revolution. It was to be symbolized by the immolation of the tsar's portrait (below), and it was to be dominated by a new political force, the Bolshevik (right).

the signal for a vigorous public movement to save the monarchy." They had grossly miscalculated, for the unrest was now too deep and widespread to be quelled by the removal of one man. To be sure, Rasputin's activities had gravely damaged the prestige of the monarchy and had driven into opposition the very social groups that normally would have supported the tsar. But by late 1916 the people of Russia — many of whom barely knew of Rasputin's existence — had become thoroughly disillusioned with the war and refused to tolerate the hardships it had caused any longer. They had endured food shortages, rising prices, devastation of Russian lands occupied by the enemy, and mounting casualties at the front. Their patience had run out.

For decades radicals had talked about revolution, but when conditions were in fact ripe for one they did not realize it. On March 8, 1917, in a spontaneous outburst of hostility against the government, thousands of people streamed into the streets of the capital (renamed Petrograd in 1914 to eliminate the German suffix "burg"), carrying red flags and banners that proclaimed "Down with the Autocracy!" The initial demonstration, held in honor of International Women's Day, a socialist occasion, seemed to be just another of the many manifestations of discontent that Petrograd had witnessed in recent months. The police dispersed the crowds that day without much difficulty.

But it soon became evident that the people had been gripped by an unprecedented militancy and that this demonstration would surpass previous ones in intensity and duration. On the following day larger crowds appeared, swollen by women from the breadlines as well as workers who had initially remained aloof. On the fourth day, when 200,000 angry people thronged the boulevards, an even more dramatic and significant event occurred: the troops not only refused to charge the marchers, they started to join their ranks. In short order the workers obtained 40,000 rifles. The government could not count on the army or on the groups that had been the mainstay of the old order.

The tsar, who had remained at the front, did not begin to understand the political situation. During the demonstrations Michael Rodzianko, president of the Duma (parliament), cabled Nicholas that the authorities in the capital faced a serious crisis and recommended that he grant concessions immediately in order to avert collapse. The impatient tsar told his court chamberlain: "That fat Rodzianko has written me some nonsense, to which I shall not even reply."

By the end of the fifth day the insurgents completed the subjugation of Petrograd. They had burned a few police stations, but resistance to them was so slight that the take-over of the vast city of 2,500,000 cost only 1,315 killed or wounded, the total number of casualties on both sides. The revolution spread rapidly after that, and by March 14 Moscow yielded to the rebels.

The next day, having been persuaded by his generals of the hopelessness of the situation, Nicholas abdicated in favor of his brother Michael. But the grand duke, sensing the unpopularity of the monarchy, declared that he would accept the crown only from a constituent assembly. This marked the end of the monarchy in Russia as well as the conclusion of the first phase of the Revolution of 1917. Before the year was out the entire political and social order would be transformed and a revolutionary Marxist party would hold power.

VIII
Nerve Center of the Soviet State

A few months after the fact, Lenin declared that the successful Bolshevik coup of November 6, 1917, "was as easy as lifting a feather." Some historians have even argued that the Bolsheviks did not seize power at all, but simply "picked it up" — for in the eight-month period following the collapse of the Romanov dynasty in March 1917, centralized authority virtually dissolved. Although the Provisional Government — led first by Prince George Lvov and then by Alexander Kerensky — granted the citizens of Russia the personal and political freedoms enjoyed by people in the most democratic countries, it proved incapable of providing them with a stable order worthy of their confidence. This failure stemmed from its inability to solve the pressing problems confronting the country.

First and foremost, the Provisional Government did not end Russia's involvement in World War I — largely because of its loyalty to the Allies and its unwillingness to capitulate to monarchical Germany. It should be added that a few ministers supported this position because they hoped to annex Constantinople after the defeat of the Central Powers, with whom Turkey was allied. As a result, a thoroughly exhausted Russia suffered one humiliating defeat after another.

The Provisional Government also blundered by not quickly holding elections for a constituent assembly, which might have provided the new regime with the legitimacy of a popular mandate. The emergence throughout the country of soviets of workers' and soldiers' deputies made such elections especially imperative. The soviets had come to exert far greater influence over the people than the government — a situation that was bound to lead to confusion and turmoil. Indeed,

the period from March to November is generally known as the era of "dual power." The responsibility of administering the country devolved on the government, but much of the time it could not enforce its decrees. The soviets — particularly the one in Petrograd — were generally heeded by the public, but they denied having any responsibility for running the country. They often disagreed with the Provisional Government about basic policies, which inevitably resulted in political paralysis during this period of national emergency.

The collapse of governmental authority affected every sphere of public life. In the army, discipline broke down: more than 2,000,000 men deserted, and between spring and autumn the 15,000,000-man army — the largest military force ever assembled — degenerated into an "enormous, exhausted, badly clothed, badly fed, embittered mob of people, united by a thirst for peace and general disillusionment." By late summer the land-hungry peasants, emboldened by success, took to pillaging estates with increasing frequency. Workers in the cities staged food riots and seized control of their factories. Finally, ethnic groups in many parts of the empire asserted their autonomy or independence. The Provisional Government found that it could do next to nothing to halt this elemental revolution from below.

Vladimir Ilich Ulyanov, better known as Lenin, founder and leader of the Bolshevik Party, was the first to appreciate the dimensions of the turbulence in Russia and to recognize that in such circumstances a small, determined group of men could attain power. When the monarchy collapsed, Lenin was in Switzerland. Desperate to return to his native country, he accepted the German government's offer to permit a few dozen Russian radicals to pass through Germany in a sealed train. The Germans were only too happy to help Lenin and his colleagues, who could be expected to make trouble for the Provisional Government and thus undermine its ability to wage war. In fact, it has been clearly established that in 1917 the Germans contributed substantial sums of money to the Bolsheviks, funds that aided the radicals immeasurably in their organizational work.

When Lenin arrived in Petrograd on April 16, 1917, he called upon the soviets to seize power and introduce "state capitalism as a transition to socialism." Not only his opponents but members of his own party repudiated his program as totally unrealistic. With characteristic tenacity, Lenin pressed for the adoption of his policies — and by October 1917 the disintegration of the country's institutions had proceeded so far that a majority of the Bolshevik Central Committee was willing to vote in favor of an insurrection. At most, Lenin's party consisted of 200,000 people, but under the circumstances this sufficed to topple the Provisional Government.

The Bolsheviks struck during the night of November 6, and with remarkably little bloodshed they took complete control of Petrograd the next day. Kerensky escaped in a car borrowed from the American legation, but his attempts to mobilize the army against the Reds came to nothing. He then fled to the West, eventually settling in New York, where he died in 1970 at the age of eighty. Although it met stiff resistance in some areas, the Revolution spread quickly. In Moscow the Bolsheviks easily occupied the Kremlin, which was strate-

gically important because of its central location and because the Arsenal contained essential arms. But immediately after the Kremlin's liberator, Ensign Berzin, led his Bolshevik forces into the citadel, they were surrounded by government troops — many of whom were *junkers* (cadets in military schools) — under the command of Colonel Riabtsev. For the time being, Berzin was prevented from delivering weapons to the Red Guards.

The Bolsheviks in Moscow were able to muster some 50,000 men against the 10,000 troops that remained loyal to the Provisional Government, yet the latter were both better trained and commanded by more experienced officers than the insurgents. These advantages turned what might have been an extraordinarily one-sided struggle into a bitter contest of unpredictable outcome. On November 9, Riabtsev threatened to bombard the Kremlin if Berzin did not immediately evacuate it. Berzin ignored the ultimatum, but for some unknown reason the government troops left the citadel intact and instead launched an offensive that drove the Bolsheviks out of the central post office, telegraph and telephone buildings, and several railway stations. At this juncture, Berzin surrendered the Kremlin on the understanding that his men would not be harmed. Colonel Riabtsev moved into the fortress and, according to some reports, violated the agreement by having a number of Red Guards shot.

The battle for Moscow was not over, however. The Bolsheviks, who still controlled the working-class districts, brought several pieces of artillery into the city and bombarded several *junker* strongholds, including the Kremlin, on November 14. After this show of

Moscow, not Petrograd, was to feel the full fury of the November coup d'etat, as an ill-trained and ill-equipped Bolshevik army (right) stormed the Kremlin itself. This second revolution was led by a Marxist firebrand named Vladimir Ilich Ulyanov. Ulyanov, who had adopted the pseudonym Lenin during his seventeen-year exile in Switzerland, is seen at left haranguing a crowd. Also included in the photograph is a rare glimpse of Leon Trotsky, who stands alongside the podium. Following Trotsky's exile and assassination, Stalin's features were substituted for those of his bitter rival in official prints of this photograph.

strength, the Red Guards stormed the Kremlin and drove Riabtsev's men out. Moscow was finally in Bolshevik hands.

The battle for Moscow had taken its toll: five hundred Bolsheviks perished, and the extent of government losses is not known. The victors honored their fallen comrades by burying them in a common grave in Red Square alongside the Kremlin wall. "The burial," a historian wrote, "was marked by a huge demonstration of workers and soldiers, who filed through Red Square with bands playing the revolutionary funeral march."

The Bolsheviks found holding onto power much more difficult than seizing it. Within a few months, Lenin and his colleagues faced such acute problems that few contemporaries, including many Bolsheviks themselves, expected the new regime to survive for long. The economy continued to deteriorate: in 1917 industrial production had declined to 33.8 per cent of what it had been in 1913, and by 1920 to 12.8 per cent. In agriculture the situation was also grim: production dropped almost one half by 1921. It has been estimated that between 1918 and 1920 more than 7,000,000 Russians died of malnutrition.

During this period civil war also menaced the Bolshevik regime. Moreover, in 1918 France, Britain, and the United States sent troops to Russia, largely for the purpose of reopening the eastern front against Germany. These foreign troops aided the four White Russian armies that were fighting the Bolsheviks in different regions of the country. Japan further complicated matters by intervening militarily in eastern Siberia to forward her own imperialistic designs. In the meantime, Lenin honored his pledge to end the war

with Germany, but at a staggering price. By the terms of the Treaty of Brest-Litovsk, signed in March 1918, Russia agreed to relinquish Poland, the Baltic states, much of Byelorussia, the Ukraine, and a strip of land on the Turkish border of Transcaucasia. These territories comprised one fourth of the empire's land mass and one third of its population. The treaty deprived Russia of both her "breadbasket" and most of her industrialized regions.

Two considerations prompted Lenin to accept these harsh conditions: first, he felt that a breathing spell might enable the regime to consolidate its position; second, he expected an imminent socialist revolution in Germany, one that would bring to power men who would renounce the treaty.

At the very moment that the Bolsheviks decided to accept Germany's peace terms, they raised a storm within the country by proposing to move the capital to Moscow, which was less exposed than Petrograd to attack either by Germany or the Whites. Several highly placed persons objected on the grounds that the move would demoralize the Petrograd workers, who were already alarmed by rumors that the government planned to hand the capital over to the Germans. According to Leon Trotsky, then second only to Lenin in power, precisely the opposite was intended. As Trotsky later recalled: "Lenin and I insisted that the transfer of the government to Moscow was to insure not only the safety of the government but of Petrograd itself. The temptation to seize the revolutionary capital and its government with it in one swift blow could not fail to appeal strongly to both Germany and the Allies. To seize a starving Petrograd without the government

would be quite another matter." After a favorable vote
in the Central Committee of the party, the leaders prepared for the move.

The Bolsheviks were so apprehensive about the pos-
sibility of a sudden attack by the Germans and the
threat of violent opposition from the citizens of the
capital that they left Petrograd secretly. Only when
Lenin and his party had almost reached their destination was the Moscow soviet informed about the impending arrival of the notables. There was no time to
organize a welcoming committee; in fact, not a single
person greeted the members of the government at the
railway station. After a brief stay in a hotel, the highest
officials settled in the Kremlin, which had endured such
neglect in recent months that it was hardly fit for occupation. But living quarters were in short supply; and, in
addition, the citadel seemed a desirable home for the
Bolshevik leaders because it could serve as a fortress in
the event of disorders. "Tomorrow, any day," one
writer noted, "the reaction, the Anarchists, or the Left
Socialist Revolutionaries might raise a revolt, and as in
the old times the new Tsars would have to fight from
behind its walls until help came."

Lenin and his colleagues moved into the Kovalevsky
Building, which prior to the Revolution had housed
tsarist officials. The first floor, previously the quarters
of the commanding officer in the Kremlin, was divided
into several small apartments, two of which Lenin and
Trotsky occupied with their families. This arrangement facilitated frequent meetings between the two
leaders of the new government. "Lenin and I met a
dozen times a day in the corridor, and called on each
other to talk things over," Trotsky tells us. "Sometimes

these talks lasted as long as ten or fifteen minutes — a
long time for us. In that period, Lenin was rather talka-
tive — judged, of course, by his standard."

Lenin's five-room apartment was reminiscent of the
unpretentious rooms he inhabited while in exile in the
West. He would not allow any of the valuable rugs or
furniture from the Kremlin's storerooms to brighten
his surroundings. Nor would he permit repairs to be
made; workers had to enter his apartment secretly during his absences to make it presentable.

As early as 1918 the Bolsheviks issued a decree providing for the preservation of national monuments and
art treasures, but they were too preoccupied with the
consolidation of authority to attend to the repair of
damaged buildings in the Kremlin. One symbolically
significant change was effected immediately, however.
According to Trotsky, "the musical clock on the Spassky [Savior Tower] was rebuilt. Now the old bells, instead of ringing out 'God Save the Czar,' slowly and
pensively rang out the 'International' [the international anthem of the Communist movement], at quar-
ter-hour intervals."

This musical change signified the Kremlin's height-
ened status under the Bolsheviks, for in addition to
serving as the seat of the Soviet government the citadel
was soon to be transformed into the headquarters of
the world revolution. In March 1919, the First Congress of the Communist International met in Moscow,
and a year later the Second Congress, representing
thirty-nine countries and five continents, assembled in
the throne room of the Palace of the Tsars. The delegates must have found it odd to sit in that luxurious
hall, for so many centuries the center of reaction, and

hear Lenin's rousing words: "Let the bourgeoisie rage; let them kill thousands of workers. The victory will be ours. The victory of the world Communist revolution is assured."

This rather fanciful prediction stemmed from the pride the Bolsheviks felt as a result of their success in establishing their rule in Russia. The Communists, as Lenin's followers were known after 1918, defeated their domestic opponents in 1919 and then initiated the first steps of a program to secure the withdrawal of foreign interventionists. The Romanovs no longer represented a threat, for Nicholas, Alexandra, and their children had been murdered on July 16, 1918.

In 1917 the Provisional Government had dispatched the entire family to Tobolsk, an isolated Siberian provincial town where the tsar was allowed to live unmolested. But in the summer of 1918 the Ural Territorial Soviet, which suddenly found itself in danger of defeat by White Guards, decided to move the royal party to Ekaterinburg — where, without the formality of a trial but with Moscow's approval, they were all shot and their bodies destroyed. According to one report, the latter action was taken "because of fear that the anti-Soviet leaders might arouse the peasants by displaying the bones of the Tsar as sacred relics." The royal family's executioners stripped all ornaments from the corpses and then transported the bodies to an abandoned mine in the village of Koptyaki, thirteen miles from Ekaterinburg. "The mine was surrounded with troops and during two days all movement was stopped on the Koptyaki highway. Great quantities of benzine and sulphuric acid were brought from Ekaterinburg; and the bodies were destroyed as

completely as possible." The executioners took the added precaution of removing the remains from the mine and dumping them in a swamp, and the president of the Ekaterinburg Soviet reported that "the corpses remained [in the swamp] and have now happily rotted."

Ironically, the death of Lenin in 1924 was marked by even more pomp than that accorded deceased monarchs in medieval Russia. Ignoring the protests of Lenin's widow and the indignation of many intellectuals, the government placed the leader's embalmed body in a temporary wooden shelter situated in Red Square opposite the Kremlin Senate Tower. Architect A. V. Shchusev then built a permanent mausoleum, one that "is organically integrated with the mass of the Kremlin and with the heart of Moscow's busiest, most modern section." The mausoleum is now the most sacred shrine in the Soviet Union, visited each year by millions of people. "For most citizens," John Gunther noted, "the visit is a profound emotional experience. Some weep; some faint; once I saw a woman go into violent hysterics."

In addition to selecting Red Square as Lenin's permanent resting place, the Bolsheviks took measures to establish themselves in the popular mind as the legitimate heirs of earlier Kremlin rulers. One government department after another moved into the citadel, and in the 1920's all the damage inflicted on Kremlin shrines during the Revolution was repaired and a wide approach was built to Red Square. A restoration commission composed of archaeologists, architects, and painters ordered the removal of many of the spurious nineteenth-century additions to the Kremlin, thus restoring its medieval appearance. In the course of this

Constantine Yuon, an established pre-Revolutionary painter, was one of the few artists to survive the upheaval. "I was working at the time while living in two worlds: the past and the present," he later noted. Those worlds meet in his canvas at right, which combines the traditional shapes of the Kremlin's ancient buildings with the bright costumes of the proletariat, massed in Red Square to celebrate the fifth anniversary of the Revolution.

work, seventeenth-century passageways under the Church of the Twelve Apostles were found, as well as the fifteenth-century windows of the Church of the Consecration of the Priests. Moreover, by removing coatings of lime and cement the artisans discovered important religious paintings in the Cathedral of the Assumption that dated from the fourteenth and fifteenth centuries.

In the 1920's, however, the Kremlin attracted world attention not so much for its artistic treasures as for the internecine power struggle that took place within its confines. By 1926 Joseph Stalin emerged as the dominant figure in the Communist Party, having overpowered the more distinguished Trotsky and Zinoviev, among others. For the next twenty-five years Stalin, who possessed a degree of power far surpassing that of any tsar, directed a "revolution from above" that transformed the Soviet Union from an underdeveloped, agricultural society into one of the most powerful industrial states in the world. Implementation of Stalin's policies involved inhumanity on a scale unknown even under the cruelest tsar. By the late 1930's, millions of citizens languished in forced labor camps and hundreds of thousands, including many of Stalin's closest collaborators, were liquidated without benefit of trial. Stalin, who seems to have suffered from acute paranoia, considered every subject a potential "enemy of the people." Only the most ruthless totalitarian regime, the dictator believed, could safeguard the new order.

In 1956 Nikita Khrushchev, a ranking official under Stalin and first secretary of the Communist Party during the period following the dictator's death in

126

Wielding powers that far exceeded those of any tsar, Joseph Stalin supervised a sweeping "revolution from above" during his twenty-five-year tenure as undisputed master of Soviet Russia's destiny. His agrarian and economic reforms dwarfed those of Peter the Great, his excesses eclipsed those of Ivan the Terrible, and his callous disregard for the well-being of his countrymen surpassed that of the last tsars of the Romanov line.

1953, revealingly described him as follows:

> Stalin was a very distrustful man, sickly suspicious; we know this from our own work with him. He could look at a man and say: "Why are your eyes so shifty today?" or "Why are you turning so much today and avoiding to look at me directly in the eyes?" The sickly suspicion created in him a general distrust even toward eminent Party workers whom he had known for years. Everywhere and in everything he saw "enemies," "two-facers," and "spies."

Khrushchev also quoted a comment made to him by Nikolai Bulganin, who was prime minister of the Russian Soviet Federative Republic, the largest united republic in the country, in 1937–38: "It has happened sometimes that a man goes to Stalin on his invitation as a friend. And, when he sits with Stalin, he does not know where he will be sent next — home or to jail."

Inside the Soviet Union the dictator's extraordinary power was justified on the ground of his infallibility and originality. At political meetings, in schools, on the radio, in literary and scholarly works, and in films Stalin was hailed as the "towering genius of all humanity." He personally claimed to be, at one and the same time, the "greatest military leader of modern times," the inspiration of all scientific advances, the judicious arbiter of the most esoteric controversies in linguistics and biology, and the sole architect of the country's economic progress.

Nothing proved to be a greater challenge to Stalin's ingenuity than the threat posed by Nazi Germany. Ultimately the Soviet dictator demonstrated remarkable leadership in coping with the threat, but initially he committed errors of judgment that can hardly be

reconciled with his vaunted reputation. In order to maintain peaceful relations between their two countries, Stalin signed a nonaggression pact with Hitler in August 1939. Publicly, the governments announced that they had simply agreed not to wage war against each other. The more significant feature of this treaty was a secret protocol that divided much of Eastern Europe between Russia and Germany and stipulated an extensive exchange of raw materials and armaments. But Hitler, who despised Bolshevism and dreamed of world conquest, considered the pact only a stopgap arrangement. By the spring of 1941 his military machine was being readied for an invasion of the Soviet Union.

Stalin refused to believe that Hitler intended to attack. In fact, Khrushchev revealed in 1956 that "Stalin ordered that no credence be given to [Churchill's] information . . . [concerning the imminence of a Nazi invasion] in order not to provoke the initiation of military operations." Incredibly, one day before the Nazi army moved across the border, Viacheslav Molotov, the foreign minister, summoned the German ambassador to his office and naïvely asked why Hitler was dissatisfied with the Soviet Union. Apparently even at this late date Stalin would have made concessions to avoid war, but the Nazi dictator was not interested in concessions. On June 22, 1941, his 3,000,000-man army launched the most ambitious campaign of conquest in recent history.

In response to this betrayal, Stalin vowed to humiliate the Germans at all costs. In an unprecedented speech delivered over the radio on July 3, he promised to "defend every inch of Soviet soil" and called on his people to follow a "scorched earth" policy in territories abandoned to the enemy. He placed the weight of his prestige solidly behind his words by stating that he personally intended to supervise the war effort.

As with the early phase of the Napoleonic campaign, the invader could not be stopped, even though the Soviet government had deployed 175 divisions near the frontier. By October 1941, the Nazis had surrounded Leningrad (as Petrograd was known after 1924) and reached Mozhaisk, sixty-five miles from Moscow. If the capital were to fall, the rest of the country might well follow. "Besides being of immense psychological importance," writes one historian, "Moscow was the center of a highly centralized regime, the hub of all Russian railways, and the transshipment point for the supplies which would soon be flowing in quantity from the United States and Britain by way of the White Sea and Vladivostok."

The German threat to the capital was so immediate that in November government departments were evacuated to Kuibyshev on the Volga. When the Muscovite population learned of the move, they were stunned. They vented their despair over the apparent decision to give the city up to the Nazis by engaging in frenzied disorders.

Stalin buoyed the spirits of the Muscovites and reassured them about the fate of their city by remaining in the Kremlin, where he stayed throughout the war. This was actually a change of routine for him. His daughter, Svetlana, disclosed that after 1933 Stalin had lived in a modest *dacha* (country cottage) in Kuntsevo, some seven miles from Moscow, even though he maintained an apartment as well as an office in the Senate

Building in the Kremlin. "After dinner," Svetlana tells us, "which generally started between six and seven in the evening and went on till eleven or twelve, he'd get into his car and go to Kuntsevo. At two or three the next day he'd be at his office."

As had been his custom prior to the outbreak of hostilities, Stalin avoided public appearances — but on November 6, 1941, the anniversary of the Revolution, he considered it necessary to inspire his army with a personal appeal. He addressed the throng in Red Square from the top of the Lenin Mausoleum:

> The enemy is not so strong as some frightened little intellectuals picture him. The devil is not so terrible as he is painted. . . . Germany cannot sustain such a strain for long. Another few months, another half a year, perhaps another year, and Hitlerite Germany must burst asunder under the pressure of her crimes.

He ended by invoking the names of Russia's pre-Bolshevik military heroes: "Let the manly images of our great ancestors — Alexander Nevsky, Prince Donskoy, Kuzma Minin, Dmitry Pozharsky, Alexander Suvurov, and Mikhail Kutuzov — inspire you in this war!"

Fortunately for the Russians, winter set in earlier than usual in 1941 — just as it had in 1812 — and the German high command made the same mistake that Napoleon had made: it sent an army into Russia that was ill-equipped to deal with severe winter weather. Nonetheless, on December 2, the Germans made a desperate effort to take Moscow, for Hitler had issued an order that "the Kremlin was to be blown up to signalize the overthrow of Bolshevism." They managed to penetrate the suburbs of Moscow, but Soviet troops, reinforced by reserves, heroically held the city. Hitler's generals, who knew their military history, pleaded with the führer to permit them to retreat, but he ignored their entreaties, dismissed several of them, and personally assumed command of the army.

Nazi triumphs during the six-month campaign had been impressive. By December 1941 the Germans occupied a vast region that included 40 per cent of the Soviet population and possessed more than one half of the country's coal, pig iron, steel, and aluminum, as well as 40 per cent of its grain supplies. Russia's industrial production in those six months declined by more than one half. But the Germans had not destroyed the Red Army or captured the capital, and the failure of Hitler's army to achieve these two goals during the initial phase of the Russian campaign proved to be a decisive turning point in the war.

The struggle lasted longer than Stalin had predicted, but by early 1943 the Germans, having lost the titanic battle of Stalingrad, could no longer mount a major offensive in Russia. Although they scored some minor victories during the next two years, they were gradually forced to withdraw in the face of one Soviet offensive after another. Russia suffered staggering losses, greater than those incurred by any other belligerent power: the official count was 7,000,000 deaths, and this figure is probably conservative. Twenty-five million people were left homeless, and the economy was a shambles. According to the best Western estimates, by 1945 the standard of living of the bulk of the Soviet population had fallen well below the 1913 level.

Yet the prestige of the Soviet Union stood higher than ever. The country had survived the Nazi on-

In an astonishing reversal of official policy, Nikita Khrushchev turned the Twentieth Party Congress in 1956 (far right) into a far-ranging attack on his predecessor, Joseph Stalin. Denouncing the "cult of personality" that surrounded the late dictator, Khrushchev announced a program of "de-Stalinization" that would expose the gross brutality and monstrous injustices of the Stalinist era. Five years later, Khrushchev presided over the opening of the Kremlin's most recent addition, the Palace of Congresses, which is topped by the ubiquitous hammer and sickle of Soviet Russia (near right).

slaught, and because Soviet armies occupied much of Eastern Europe, Stalin could insist on substantial annexations of territory and on the installation of Communist regimes in Albania, Bulgaria, East Germany, Poland, Rumania, Yugoslavia, and — somewhat later — Czechoslovakia. Thus the spread of Bolshevism took place as a result of a devastating war, not the collapse of capitalism, as had been predicted by Marxists. Adolf Hitler, who had vowed to destroy communism, became the unwitting agent of its greatest advances.

Not surprisingly, Stalin's personal authority within the Soviet Union remained unchallenged, and under his aegis the economic reconstruction of the country began. Despite the people's sacrifices, the dictator took no steps to loosen his totalitarian grip. He looked upon Ivan the Terrible as the model of the ideal ruler, because of all the tsars he alone had possessed the foresight to introduce a monopoly on foreign trade. Ivan could be considered "a true socialist," Stalin's own historical forerunner. In 1947 the dictator ordered a producer to make a film showing the sixteenth-century tsar as a "great and wise ruler." This incident, writes a student of Soviet affairs, "is full of implications for an understanding of Soviet Russia's history in the Stalin period."

In the winter of 1952–53 there were ominous signs that Stalin planned a new massive purge of the party and the liquidation of a number of his closest collaborators. The Soviet Union appeared to be on the verge of a cataclysm reminiscent of the horrors of the late 1930's, but on March 5, 1953, before the plans could be implemented, the dictator died of a stroke. Rumors circulated that he had been the victim of foul play, but

these have never been substantiated. Many people simply refused to believe that the seventy-three-year-old dictator could have died of that unnatural cause of death among Soviet leaders, old age.

On March 9 Stalin's body was placed next to Lenin's in the mausoleum, "amidst pomp and solemnity, to the accompaniment of the mournful tolling of thousands of church bells, the piercing sound of factory whistles, and doleful funeral music emanating from millions of loudspeakers throughout the land." Fearful of disorder, Stalin's successors urged the masses to avoid confusion and panic. They also sought to appease the people by granting amnesty to certain categories of political prisoners. A collective leadership was established, and although some members of that ruling group have exercised more power than others, no single autocrat, glorified in Byzantine fashion, has emerged.

The new rulers have not instituted a democratic order by any means; the country is still run by one party, and expressions of dissent are still punishable offenses. Yet the terroristic regime has been modified: far fewer forced labor camps exist today than did in the 1940's, and the Soviet citizen no longer lives in the same dread of the political police. The struggles for power at the top of the Communist Party hierarchy no longer result in the physical extermination of the vanquished. In sum, it might be said that the totalitarian controls over the population have been loosened but not removed.

One early sign of this loosening was that the Kremlin, which had been carefully guarded and closed to the public throughout the Stalin era, ceased to be a fortress sealed off from the people. A few months after the

dictator's death the government reduced the police cordon around the citadel, and late in 1953 Soviet ministers began to move out of the Kremlin and into houses in Moscow. In 1954 the Kremlin was opened to the public for special occasions and a year later it was declared a national museum accessible to visitors.

Shortly after these changes, Khrushchev inaugurated a dramatic campaign of "de-Stalinization." At the Twentieth Party Congress in 1956 he astonished the delegates by recounting many of the horrors of Stalinism and repudiating the "cult of personality." For the first time a responsible Soviet leader in power admitted that Stalin had perpetrated the monstrous crimes of which the West had long accused him. Even so, it is important to note that Khrushchev condemned only the excesses of the Stalin era — without questioning the overall system of government. In fact, he emphasized his conviction that the dictator's crimes were not the "deeds of a giddy despot." Admittedly, Stalin had been excessively extolled. However, Stalin had "doubtlessly performed great services to the Party, to the working class, and to the international workers' movement." Khrushchev concluded by calling for a complete restoration of the "Leninist principles of Soviet socialist democracy, expressed in the Constitution of the Soviet Union."

Although the Soviet leader tried to avoid totally repudiating Stalinist policies, his revelations caused a sensation. Commentators on Soviet affairs are still not agreed as to his motives for exposing the horrors of the 1940's; after all, Khrushchev himself risked being called to account, for he had occupied high positions under Stalin. He was probably motivated by the realization

that the Soviet people and the citizens of other Communist countries yearned for an end to the terror associated with the Stalinist cult. In an account of his travels in Russia in 1956, John Gunther relates a widely circulated joke that tends to support this interpretation. According to Moscow wags, when Yugoslavia's Marshal Tito visited the mausoleum, he saluted the structure with a hand over one eye — so that he could see Lenin but not Stalin.

The duration and intensity of the anti-Stalinist campaign lends even greater weight to this interpretation. The campaign reached its highest — and certainly its most bizarre — point at the Twenty-second Party Congress in 1961. On that occasion D. A. Lazurkina, a longtime party member who had spent many years in a forced labor camp, strode to the platform and delivered these remarkable words:

I always carry Ilyich [Lenin] in my heart, always, comrades, and at the most difficult moments the only thing that carried me through was that I had Ilyich in my heart, and could consult with him as to what I must do. I consulted with Ilyich yesterday, it was as if he were alive and standing in front of me, and he said: "It is unpleasant for me to be side by side with Stalin, who brought so many troubles upon the party."

The congress, which dared not offend the sensibilities of its revolutionary hero, promptly passed a resolution acknowledging that it was "inappropriate to retain the sarcophagus containing the coffin of I. V. Stalin in the Mausoleum," citing Stalin's "serious violation of the behests of Lenin, his abuse of power, his mass repressions against honest Soviet people, and other actions in the period of the cult of personality." The next day

This telescopic view of Lenin's squat, red granite tomb (center opposite) is framed by the Historical Museum (near right) and the Corner Arsenal Tower (far right). Between them lies the broad expanse of Red Square, dominated by the snow-capped domes of Saint Basil the Blessed. Surmounted by a red star, the Savior Tower stands today, as it did five centuries ago, as the principal entrance to the Russian nation's political and spiritual heart.

Stalin's body was removed and reburied in a plot behind the Mausoleum near the Kremlin wall.

In order to help eradicate the dictator's memory, the congress renamed many cities. Thus, for example, Stalino became Donetsk; Stalinabad, Diushambe, and world-renowned Stalingrad, where Hitler's army suffered its greatest defeat, Volgograd. Soviet wits circulated the story that their deceased leader had sent the delegates a telegram promising cooperation with all their decisions. The message bore the following signature: "Joseph Vissarionovich Volgin."

These astonishing deliberations were held in the Kremlin's newest structure, the Palace of Congresses, which had been completed in 1961. Its main hall accommodates six thousand people and is used both for major party functions and for theatrical and musical performances. Numerous loudspeakers have been installed throughout the hall to overcome the acoustical problems that arise from its size. Its sheer size also explains why one Western observer stated that the hall "is a disaster for performer-audience contact." From an architectural point of view, the Palace of Congresses is one of the Russian capital's more interesting and sophisticated recent achievements. A thoroughly contemporary and austerely elegant building, it somehow harmonizes with the medieval structures that predominate in the Kremlin. Moreover, it is a welcome change from the drab edifices that were generally erected during Stalin's regime.

Thus, the structures that constitute the modern Kremlin exemplify the full range of artistic styles that have prevailed during its eight-hundred-year existence. During much of that time, the events that took place behind its walls were shrouded in mystery. Time and again in our account of its history we have had to acknowledge ignorance or uncertainty, for nearly all of the Kremlin's occupants took precautions to conceal both their actions and the reasons for them. During the last sixteen years the Kremlin has been physically open to the public, but the wholly private way in which Soviet leaders reach their decisions continues to baffle political observers.

To the student of Russian history the paucity of indisputable information about developments within the Kremlin can be frustrating. Yet the very mysteriousness that has characterized the citadel makes it a particularly fascinating subject for study, as does its uniqueness among man's creations. Nowhere else does there exist an architectural complex that can rival the Kremlin's long and variegated history, its importance in creating a vast empire, and its present position as the political nerve center of one of the modern world's two mightiest powers.

ГЕРБЪ ЧЕРНОЙ ГОРЫ

THE KREMLIN
IN LITERATURE

Vasili III, Grand Prince of Muscovy from 1505 to 1533, was the son of Ivan the Great and the father of Ivan the Terrible. Oddly enough — considering his lineage — Vasili's reign was neither distinguished nor notorious but was instead a tranquil and uneventful interregnum between the reigns of the two mighty Ivans. During the middle years of Vasili's tenure, Baron Sigismund von Herberstein arrived in Moscow to serve as ambassador from the Holy Roman Empire. The fastidious and cultivated baron was overwhelmed by the squalor, the backwardness, and the filth he encountered, and his portrait of the Russian capital — the earliest known description of the city — is a rather unflattering one.

This city is so broad and spacious, and so very dirty, that bridges have been constructed here and there in the highways and streets and in the other more distinguished parts. There is a fortress in it built of burnt tiles, which on one side is washed by the Mosqwa [Moscow River] and on the other by the River Neglima [Neglinnaia]. The Neglima flows from certain marshes, but is so blocked up before the city around the upper part of the fortress, that it comes out like stagnant water, and running down thence, it fills the moats of the fortress, in which are some mills, and at length, as I have said, is joined by the Mosqwa under the fortress itself. The fortress is so large, that it not only contains the very extensive and magnificently built stone palace of the prince, but the metropolitan bishop, the brothers of the prince, the peers, and a great many others, have spacious houses of wood within it. Besides these, it contains many churches, so that from its size it might almost be taken for a city. This fortress was at first surrounded only by oaks, and up to the time of the Grand Duke Ivan Danielovich [Ivan I] was small and mean in appearance. It was he, who, by the persuasion of Peter the metropolitan, first transferred the imperial residence to this place. Peter had originally selected that place from love of one Alexius, who was buried there, and who is said to have been famous for miracles; and after his death, being buried in this place, miracles were likewise done at his tomb, so that the place itself acquired such a celebrity, from a certain notion of its sacredness and religious character, that all the princes who succeeded Ivan thought that the seat of empire ought to be held there. For on the death of Ivan, his son of the same name retained his seat there; and after him, Dimitry; and after Dimitry, that Vasiley, who married the daughter of Withold, and left behind him Vasiley the Blind. Of him was born Ivan, the father of that prince, at whose court I was ambassador, and who first surrounded the fortress with a wall; and his descendants, nearly thirty years after, have brought the work to completion. The ramparts and battlements of this fortress, as well as the prince's palace, were built of brick, in the Italian style, by Italians, whom the prince had sent for from Italy with the offer of large remuneration. There are also, as I have said, many churches in it, nearly all of wood, except the two handsomest, which are built of brick. One of these is consecrated to the Blessed Virgin, the other to St. Michael. In the church of the Blessed Virgin are buried the bodies of the two archbishops who were the cause of the prince's transferring thither the seat of empire and the metropolis; and principally on that account they have been enrolled among the number of the saints. The other church is used as a burial-place for the princes. There were also many churches, being built of stone, at the time I was there.

SIGISMUND VON HERBERSTEIN
Notes Upon Russia, c. 1540

Johann Georg Korb, a twenty-eight-year-old secretary at the Austrian embassy in Moscow, had been at his post for little more than four months when the twenty-six-year-old tsar cut short an extended tour of Western Europe and hastened home to suppress the streltsy *revolt of 1698. The day after the impetuous young ruler returned, he instituted the first of the sweeping reforms that were to wrench his country out of its feudal backwardness and turn it toward Europe. To underscore the earnestness of his intentions, Peter began by personally shaving off the long beards of his boyars — an event Korb was careful to record in his diary. Indeed, the young Austrian's journal was so complete and so detailed that its publication caused a major Continental scandal. To ease the diplomatic tension generated by Korb's unrestrained narrative, Emperor Leopold I of Austria ordered the destruction of all unsold copies of the work, and in Moscow a copy was publicly burned by the state executioner. So effective was Peter's campaign against Korb's work that only ten copies of the diary have survived.*

5th September, 1698.

The report of the Czar's arrival had spread through the city. The Boyars and principal Muscovites flocked in numbers at an early hour to the place where it had become known he had spent the night, to pay their court. Great was the crowd of congratulators, who came to prove by the promptitude of their obsequiousness the constancy of their spotless loyalty to their sovereign. Although the chief ambassador, Francis, son of James Lefort, would receive nobody that day, alleging the fatigue occasioned by such long and uninterrupted traveling, nevertheless his Majesty the Czar received all that came, with an alacrity that showed as if he wished to be beforehand with his subjects in eagerness. Those who, according to the fashion of that country, would cast themselves upon the ground to worship majesty, he lifted up graciously from their groveling posture, and embraced with a kiss, such as is only due among private friends. If the razor, that plied promiscuously among the beards of those present, can be forgiven the injury it did, the Muscovites may truly reckon that day among the happiest of their lives. Knes Alexis Simonowicz Schachin, General-in-Chief of the Czar's troops, was the first who submitted the encumbrance of his long beard to the razor.

Nor can they consider it any disgrace, as their sovereign is the first to show the example — their sovereign to whose wish or command they deem it a holy and religious command to devote their lives. Nor was there anybody left to laugh at the rest. They were all born to the same fate. Nothing but superstitious awe for his office exempted the Patriarch. Prince Lehugowicz Tzerkasky was let off out of reverence for his advanced years, and Tichon Nikitowicz Stresnow out of the honor due to one who had been guardian to the Czarine. All the rest had to conform to the guise of foreign nations, and the razor eliminated the ancient fashion. In speaking of the foreign sovereigns he had visited, he made honorable mention of the King of Poland. "I prize him more than the whole of you together," (he was addressing his Boyars and magnates that were present) "and that not because of his royal preëminence over you, but merely because I like him."

Such was the effect of the three days during which [Peter had] enjoyed the King's society. . . .

6th September, 1698.

The Czar inspected his troops at exercise; and seeing at a glance how backward they were as compared with other soldiers, he went himself through

Nineteenth-century watercolors from Solntzev's Costumes of the Russian State *illustrate pages 139–59 of* The Kremlin in Literature.

all the attitudes and movements of the manual exercise, teaching them by his own motions how they should endeavor to form their heavy clumsy bodies. Tired at last with the uncouth horde, he went off with a bevy of Boyars to a dinner which he had ordered at his Ambassador Lefort's. Salvos of artillery mingled with the shouts of the drinkers, and the pleasures of the table were protracted to a late hour of the evening. Then, taking advantage of the shades of night, attended by a very few of those in whom he reposes most confidence, he went into the Castle of the Kremlin, where he indulged a father's affection in seeing his darling little son, kissed him thrice, and leaving many other pledges of endearment, returned to his wooden dwelling in Bebraschentsko, flying the sight of his wife, the Czarine, whom he dislikes with a loathing of old date.

The Czar's ministry had a friendly hint given to the Lord Envoy to abstain a little from appearing in public, and not allow those of his household to go out of doors too much; that it was necessary to yield so much to custom in order not to risk the high esteem which he had hitherto won from everybody.

8th September, 1698.

His majesty the Czar was reported to have graciously favored his most serene wife with a secret conversation of four hours' duration in a strange house, but the rumor was utterly false. . . .

11th September, 1698.

The Russians begin their year, according to the old calendar, in the first of September, for they reckon the number of years from the creation of the world. Moreover, a venerable custom used to mark this day among the Russians by a great and ancient solemnity. In the most spacious courtyard of the Castle of the Kremlin, two thrones, most richly adorned, used to be erected for the Czar and the Patriarchs. The latter in the splendor of his pontificals, the former in his royal robes, sat in these thrones, adding by the grandeur of this attire to that reverence for majesty which, even without that outward adornment, the people looked up to as a kind of divinity that only seldom appears. After a solemn benediction given by the Patriarch, the congratulations of the magnates and other chief persons were borne to the Czar, who returned thanks with a nod for their good wishes. The absence of the Czar for many years had occasioned the intermission of these rites, and, with the new-fangled ambition of our days, they were left unrevived as things worn-out and obsolete. It was considered that the worship of by-gone generations was needlessly superstitious in allowing majesty to be wrapped up with so many sacred rites. Nevertheless a jolly inauguration of the year took place in a banquet prepared with royal munificence at the house of General-in-Chief Schachin. A crowd of Boyars, scribes, and military officers, almost incredible, was assembled there, and among them were several common sailors, with whom the Czar repeatedly mixed, divided apples, and even honored one of them by calling him brother. A salvo of twenty-five great guns marked each toast. Nor could the irksome offices of the barber check the festivities of the day, though it was well known he was enacting the part of jester by appointment at the Czar's court. It was of evil omen to make show of reluctance as the razor approached the chin, and was to be forthwith punished with a boxing on the ears. In this way, between mirth and the wine-cup, many were admonished by this insane ridicule to abandon the olden guise.

JOHANN GEORG KORB
Diary, c. 1700

ROYAL RECOLLECTIONS

Sophia Augusta Frederica of Anhalt-Zerbst and her parents were sitting at their dining-room table on the night of January 6, 1744, when a courier arrived with a vitally important imperial missive. That letter, which was addressed to Sophia's mother, proposed a political marriage between "the Princess, Your eldest daughter" and the heir-apparent to the Russian throne, Grand Duke Peter. Traveling incognito to preserve their ill-kept secret, the fourteen-year-old German princess and her mother set out for Russia. Ten days after her arrival in Saint Petersburg, Sophia — the future Catherine the Great — fell gravely ill, and it was not until April 21, her fifteenth birthday, that the bride-to-be was able to rise from her sickbed. As soon as she felt well enough to travel, Sophia journeyed on to Moscow, where she was formally betrothed to the man she would marry and depose within two decades. Years later Catherine recorded her first impressions of Russia in her Memoirs.

On April 21st, the day on which I was fifteen years old, I was able to stand on my feet and receive congratulations. The Empress had me put on rouge on account of the striking paleness which I still retained. . . .

On the day before St. Peter's, I made my confession of faith and received communion in the public royal chapel in the presence of a vast crowd of people. I read in the Russian language, which I did not at all understand, quite fluently and with a faultless accent fifty quarter-pages, and recited afterwards from memory the symbol of faith. The Archbishop of Novgorod and the Abbess of a nunnery, who stood in the odor of sanctity, were my godparents. I received the name which I now bear, solely for the reason that my former name [Sophia] was hated on account of the plots of the sister of Peter the Great, who had been called the same. From the moment of my change of faith I was prayed for in all the churches.

In the evening we went incognito to the Kremlin, an old castle, which served the Czars as a residence. I was lodged in a room so high that you could hardly see the people who went along the foot of the wall.

Early in the morning of the day afterwards, St. Peter's day, on which my betrothal was to take place, I received as a present from the Empress her portrait set with diamonds, and a moment afterwards that of the Grand Duke, equally valuable.

Immediately afterwards I was taken to the Empress, who, with the crown upon her head and wearing the imperial mantle, set forth under a canopy of massive silver borne by eight Major-Generals. The Grand Duke and I followed her, after us came my mother, the Princess of Homburg, and the other ladies according to their rank. Incidentally, from the moment of my change of faith it was arranged that I should have precedence over my mother, although I was not yet betrothed.

We descended the famous stairway, known as the Krasnoe Kryltso, crossed the square and proceeded on foot to the cathedrals, while the regiments of the Guard formed a lane. The clergy received us as usual. The Empress took the Grand Duke and me by the hand and led us to a platform covered with velvet in the middle of the church. There the Archbishop Ambrosius of Novgorod betrothed us and the Empress exchanged the rings. The ring which I received from the Grand Duke was worth twelve thousand rubles, and the one, which he received from me, fourteen thousand.

After the mass, the cannons fired a salute. At mid-day the Empress dined with the Grand Duke and me on the throne in the room which is called the "Granovitaya Palata." My mother had demanded to be present at the dinner, whereupon they told her she could only have a place among the other ladies, but she demanded to be seated on the throne only one step lower. When Lord Tyrawley heard that he declared that, as the representative of a crowned head, he would also take his place there. So a table was set for her in the place from which the Princesses of the Czar's family used to look on during ceremonial occasions; that is a little room high up behind a glass wall. She ate there, so to speak, incognito, for the Princess of Homburg and several other ladies took part.

In the evening a ball took place at the foot of the throne, on a carpet on which, of the ladies, only the Empress, my mother, myself, and the Princess of Hessen danced; of the gentlemen, only the Grand Duke, the Ambassadors of England, Holstein, Denmark, and the Prince of Hessen. The rest of the company danced on the right. We were almost smothered with the heat and the crowds. The chamber is so constructed that a great pillar supports the arch in the middle and takes up almost a quarter of the room. After the ball we returned to the Annenhof Palace, behind the German Sloboda which we occupied.

Some time later the peace with Sweden was celebrated with a public festival. Immediately afterwards we departed for Kiev.

CATHERINE THE GREAT
Memoirs, c. 1756

AN IMPERIAL CORONATION

Mrs. John A. Logan, wife of the Civil War general and U.S. senator, had been widowed for nearly a decade when she set out on her grand tour of Europe in 1896. Mrs. Logan's entourage, which included twenty-one-year-old Kate Koon and her younger sister, reached Paris by early spring — and it was during their stay in the French capital that young Kate and the other women received formal invitations to the coronation of the last Tsar of All the Russias, Nicholas II, and his recent bride, Alexandra Feodorovna. In a series of letters to her family, the impressed and irrepressible Miss Koon recorded the elaborate festivities preceding the ceremony and the glittering panoply of the imperial procession itself.

Moscow, Tuesday, May 26, 1896

Dear Papa and Mama:

The grandest day of my life was also the most important day in the life of Nicholas II, the Czar of the Russians. According to the Julian calendar used in Russia this is May 14, for there is a difference of twelve days between it and the Gregorian calendar used in the United States.

I am going back to the very beginning and tell you everything, for it was all so wonderful, so grand and so royal. We had been greatly exercised about our invitations to the coronation, but as nothing was to be known until the last moment we had to wait. We expected to get our tickets for seats in the tribune [viewing stand] from the Legation, where they were to be sent by the Russian Master of Ceremonies. Mrs. Logan knew one of the aid-de-camps of the Czar, and he came to see us yesterday to find out about our arrangements. I had to do the talking to him as he spoke only French and Russian. He was as nice as he could be and promised to do what he could for us, if we did not succeed in getting our tickets at the Embassy.

Last night a dinner was given by Minister and Mrs. Breckenridge, and we

were all invited. Almost as soon as we got there each of the thirty guests was presented with a large envelope in which were two admission cards and a large invitation in the name of the Emperor for us to come to the square of the Cathedral in the Kremlin and have seats in the tribune of the Diplomatic Corps. On one of the cards was printed, *"Traine de cour* [court train]."

These three words created almost more excitement among us than did the invitation itself. We had not unpacked or even seen or tried on our trains, and the fact that at six o'clock in the morning we must have them on and be ready to leave the house caused us to leave the dinner and the delightful guests, including Richard Harding Davis . . . and other interesting people, and go home early to try on our finery so that there would be no hitches in the morning, for as it was we must get up at four-thirty. Some one had told us that the gates of the Kremlin would be closed at seven, while others said not until eight, and, in spite of the fact that our invitations told us to be at the "stairs of the Winter Garden of the Palace at 8:15," Mrs. Logan said she was sure we would not get in if we waited until that time and that we must go early. We spent about half the night getting our clothes in readiness and wondering how we were going to manage our trains, which were four yards long from the shoulders. . . .

At four o'clock I woke up to find the promise of a glorious, warm day, and I got up for good at five (not 4:30 for we begged off a half hour), had breakfast at six, ate as many boiled eggs as I possibly could, put on as many warm clothes as possible, saw that my blue satin train, with its bunches of pink poppies and its ruche of blue tulle was nicely hung over my left arm, and then tucked myself into the carriage with three other equally corpulent bundles of silk and satin, and away we went. Unfortunately we went to the wrong gate, and when finally we alighted from the carriage we had to sachet [sashay] up and down rows of men, through masses of people and past tribunes or stands full of very plainly dressed women, until we could find some one who understood what particular place our tickets called for. We felt rather odd being so over dressed until finally some man, glittering with gold, escorted us to our seats and we found we had the best place in the entire Kremlin enclosure.

The tribune, in the second story of which we sat, faced the Kremlin square, which was surrounded by three churches, the famous Red Staircase leading to the palace and the stands which had been erected in all the possible spaces, completed the surroundings of the square. There was almost no one in the Diplomatic tribune when we arrived, although it was a little after seven. We got our seats in the second row, and when we had settled ourselves with our trains heaped in our laps, we began to take in the gorgeous sight spread out before us. . . .

. . . Already the square was filling with people, and more kept coming in from all sides. The gorgeous red, white and gold uniforms of the guards, who lined the edges of the crimson carpet wherever it was laid were quite put to shame as the many representatives of the various oriental countries began to arrive. . . . There were Persians, each wearing a black fez, Turks with their red ones, Bokharans with white or colored turbans and gowns of the richest stuffs, Koreans with the queerest black headdresses, Hussars with gold and fur trimmed coats hanging from their shoulders, and Caucasians in their long red coats. From the steppes of Siberia there were men whose hats were like sombreros. . . .

The priests and the metropolitans who are the next after the Czar in rank in the Greek church, robed in cloth of gold, and one wearing a gold and diamond mitre, passed into the Cathedral through a small side door. Soon the gentlemen of the imperial household filed into the church; then a large body of deputies from the different towns marched in. We wondered how the small church was going to hold all of them, together with the royal guests who had not yet gone in. The question was soon solved, for by watching another side door we could see the two processions file out. The diplomats and their wives began to descend the Red Staircase and were escorted by some of the high men of the court. A canopy of gold cloth with yellow, white and black ostrich feathers in great bunches on the top was carried to the foot of the stairway, and following a procession of brilliantly dressed men, the Dowager Empress appeared attired in a gown of embroidered white velvet, her long train carried aloft by a dozen men. . . .

The young Czar and his wife now appeared on the stairway. He was dressed in a blue uniform with a red ribbon across his breast. At his side was the beautiful Czarina in white wearing her red ribbon and around her neck were magnificent pearls. The people were wild with joy when the young couple came in sight. The Czar stepped first under a larger and more magnificent canopy than that under which his mother had moved. The Czarina walked behind him under the same canopy as they moved slowly to the door of the Cathedral, where they stopped for a long time for holy anointing and for prayers. The priests who had been around in the square throwing holy water upon the people were all in place now in the procession which moved to the door of the tiny Cathedral of the Assumption. . . .

We tried . . . to create a mental picture of the way the Czar's mantle was put about his shoulders and how he put his own crown on his head after receiving the benediction from the priests. When he had taken his sceptre and the globe into his hand, he seated himself for a moment upon his throne. . . . His next step was to take off his own crown and place it for a moment upon the Czarina's head, then replace it upon his own and take her small one and crown her. Her mantle was then put on, the bells and the cannon proclaimed to the people the coronation, and so loud was the noise I wonder you did not hear it. I suppose the telegraph announced the news to you across the seas. . . .

. . . The cheering began near the side door and heralded the coming of the newly crowned pair. . . . The Emperor's crown of diamonds flashed like a veritable sun, as he walked under his awning followed by the Empress. The procession passed from our sight for a few moments while the royal couple showed themselves to the people in the tribunes back of the square. We had not long to wait for they soon came back and went to the second cathedral, there to kiss the relics and "salute the tombs of their ancestors." Then they passed to the next church to do the same. At the entrance to each cathedral they were met by a group of priests who went in with them. When they had performed these duties their majesties left their canopy at the foot of the Red Staircase and ascended it amid the cheers of the people. At the top they turned for the people to catch the last glimpse of them, then they passed into the palace, and that part of the coronation festivities was at an end.

KATE KOON BOVEY
Russian Coronation, 1896

MOSCOW IN FLAMES

War and Peace, Count Leo Tolstoi's monumental account of Napoleon's invasion of Russia, builds around, rather than upon, the events of 1812. The military campaign itself receives only secondary consideration; its impact upon Tolstoi's characters is plainly the author's prime concern. As a result, the pivotal episode of the entire campaign — the utter breakdown of military discipline that occurred during the Grand Army's five-week occupation of Moscow, a breakdown that forced Napoleon to abandon his ambitious enterprise and retreat ignominiously across the blizzard-swept steppes — passes almost unnoticed. The passage that describes the withdrawal of the French army concludes with an entirely credible explanation of why Moscow burned.

Toward four o'clock in the afternoon Murat's troops were entering Moscow. In front rode a detachment of Württemberg hussars and behind them rode the King of Naples himself accompanied by a numerous suite.

About the middle of the Arbát Street, near the Church of the Miraculous Icon of St. Nicholas, Murat halted to await news from the advanced detachment as to the condition in which they had found the citadel, *le Kremlin*.

Around Murat gathered a group of those who had remained in Moscow. They all stared in timid bewilderment at the strange, long-haired commander dressed up in feathers and gold.

"Is that their Tsar himself? He's not bad!" low voices could be heard saying.

An interpreter rode up to the group.

"Take off your cap . . . your caps!" These words went from one to another in the crowd. The interpreter addressed an old porter and asked if it was far to the Krémlin. The porter, listening in perplexity to the unfamiliar Polish accent and not realizing that the interpreter was speaking Russian, did not understand what was being said to him and slipped behind the others.

Murat approached the interpreter and told him to ask where the Russian army was. One of the Russians understood what was asked and several voices at once began answering the interpreter. A French officer, returning from the advanced detachment, rode up to Murat and reported that the gates of the citadel had been barricaded and that there was probably an ambuscade there.

"Good!" said Murat and, turning to one of the gentlemen in his suite, ordered four light guns to be moved forward to fire at the gates.

The guns emerged at a trot from the column following Murat and advanced up the Arbát. When they reached the end of the Vozdvízhenka Street they halted and drew up in the Square. Several French officers superintended the placing of the guns and looked at the Krémlin though field glasses.

The bells in the Krémlin were ringing for vespers, and this sound troubled the French. They imagined it to be a call to arms. A few infantrymen ran to the Kutáfyev Gate. Beams and wooden screens had been put there, and two musket shots rang out from under the gate as soon as an officer and men began to run toward it. A general who was standing by the guns shouted some words of command to the officer, and the latter ran back again with his men.

The sound of three more shots came from the gate.

One shot struck a French soldier's foot, and from behind the screens came the strange sound of a few voices shouting. Instantly as at a word of command the expression of cheerful serenity on the faces of the French general, officers, and men changed to one of determined concentrated readiness for strife and suffering. To all of them from the marshal to the least soldier, that place was not the Vozdvízhenka, Mokhaváya, or Kutáfyev Street, nor the Tróitsa Gate (places familiar in Moscow), but a new battlefield which would probably prove sanguinary. And all made ready for that battle. The cries from the gates ceased. The guns were advanced, the artillerymen blew the ash off their linstocks, and an officer gave the word "Fire!" This was followed by two whistling sounds of canister shot, one after another. The shot rattled against the stone of the gate and upon the wooden beams and screens, and two wavering clouds of smoke rose over the Square.

A few instants after the echo of the reports resounding over the stone-built Krémlin had died away the French heard a strange sound above their head. Thousands of crows rose above the walls and circled in the air, cawing and noisily flapping their wings. Together with that sound came a solitary human cry from the gateway and amid the smoke appeared the figure of a bareheaded man in a peasant's coat. He grasped a musket and took aim at the French. "Fire!" repeated the officer once more, and the reports of a musket and of two cannon shots were heard simultaneously. The gate was again hidden by smoke.

Nothing more stirred behind the screens and the French infantry soldiers and officers advanced to the gate. In the gateway lay three wounded and four dead. Two men in peasant coats ran away at the foot of the wall, toward the Známenka.

"Clear that away!" said the officer, pointing to the beams and the corpses, and the French soldiers, after dispatching the wounded, threw the corpses over the parapet. . . .

Murat was informed that the way had been cleared. The French entered the gates and began pitching their camp in the Senate Square. Out of the windows of the Senate House the soldiers threw chairs into the Square for fuel and kindled fires there. . . .

Though tattered, hungry, worn out, and reduced to a third of their original number, the French entered Moscow in good marching order. It was a weary and famished, but still a fighting and menacing army. But it remained an army only until its soldiers had dispersed into their different lodgings. As soon as the men of the various regiments began to disperse among the wealthy and deserted houses, the army was lost forever and there came into being something nondescript, neither citizens nor soldiers but what are known as marauders. When five weeks later these same men left Moscow, they no longer formed an army. They were a mob of marauders, each carrying a quantity of articles which seemed to him valuable or useful. The aim of each man when he left Moscow was no longer, as it had been, to conquer, but merely to keep what he had acquired. Like a monkey which puts its paw into the narrow neck of a jug, and having seized a handful of nuts will not open its fist for fear of losing what it holds, and therefore perishes, the French when they left Moscow had inevitably to perish because they carried their loot with them, yet to abandon what they had stolen was as impossible for them as it is for the monkey to open its paw and let go of its nuts. Ten minutes after each regiment had entered a Moscow district, not a soldier or officer was left. Men in military uniforms and Hessian boots could be seen through the windows, laughing and walking through the rooms. In cellars and storerooms similar men were busy among the provisions, and in the yards unlocking or breaking open coach house and stable doors, lighting fires in kitchens and kneading and baking bread with rolled-up sleeves. . . .

Order after order was issued by the French commanders that day forbidding the men to disperse about the town, sternly forbidding any violence to the inhabitants or any looting, and announcing a roll call for that very evening. But despite all these measures the men, who had till then constituted an army, flowed all over the wealthy, deserted city with its comforts and plentiful supplies. As a hungry herd of cattle keeps well together when crossing a barren field, but gets out of hand and at once disperses uncontrollably as soon as it reaches rich pastures, so did the army disperse all over the wealthy city.

No residents were left in Moscow, and the soldiers — like water percolating through sand — spread irresistibly through the city in all directions from the Krémlin into which they had first marched. The cavalry, on entering a merchant's house that had been abandoned and finding there stabling more than sufficient for their horses, went on, all the same, to the next house which seemed to them better. Many of them appropriated several houses, chalked their names on them, and quarreled and even fought with other companies for them. Before they had had time to secure quarters the soldiers ran out into the streets to see the city and, hearing that everything had been abandoned, rushed to places where valuables were to be had for the taking. The officers followed to check the soldiers and were involuntarily drawn into doing the same. In Carriage Row carriages had been left in the shops, and generals flocked there to select *calèches* and coaches for themselves. The few inhabitants who had remained invited commanding officers into their houses, hoping thereby to secure themselves from being plundered. There were masses of wealth and there seemed no end to it. All around the quarters occupied by the French were other regions still unexplored and unoccupied where, they thought, yet greater riches might be found. And Moscow engulfed the army ever deeper and deeper. When water is spilled on dry ground both the dry ground and the water disappear and mud results; and in the same way the entry of the famished army into the rich and deserted city resulted in fires and looting and the destruction of both the army and the wealthy city.

The French attributed the Fire of Moscow *au patriotisme féroce de Rostopchine* [to Moscow Governor Fedor Rostopchín's ferocious patriotism], the Russians to the barbarity of the French. In reality, however, it was not, and could not be, possible to explain the burning of Moscow by making any individual, or any group of people, responsible for it. Moscow was burned because it found itself in a position in which any town built of wood was bound to burn, quite apart from whether it had, or had not, a hundred and thirty inferior fire engines. Deserted Moscow had to burn as inevitably as a heap of shavings has to burn on which sparks continually fall for several days. A town built of wood, where scarcely a day passes without conflagrations when the house owners are in residence and a police force is present, cannot help burning when its inhabitants have left it and it is occupied by soldiers who smoke pipes, make campfires of the Senate chairs in the Senate Square, and cook themselves meals twice a day. In peacetime it is only necessary to billet troops in the villages of any district and the number of fires in that district immediately increases. How much then must the probability of fire be increased in an abandoned, wooden town where foreign troops are quartered. "*Le patriotisme féroce de Rostopchine*" and the barbarity of the French were not to blame in the matter. Moscow was set on fire by the soldiers' pipes, kitchens, and campfires, and by the carelessness of enemy soldiers occupying houses they did not own.

LEO TOLSTOI
War and Peace, 1866

Aleksandr Sergeevich Pushkin, preeminent poet of nineteenth-century Russia, treated the burning of Moscow in an equally individual fashion in his long, semi-autobiographical verse-novel, Eugene Onegin. *In Pushkin's romanticized version, the defiant city simply consumed itself rather than capitulate to Napoleon. As the flames began to lick the walls of his Kremlin headquarters, the rebuffed French emperor was forced to repair to Petrovskiy Castle on the outskirts of the city. And it was from that vantage that the would-be conqueror watched "the formidable flame" reduce the abandoned capital to smoking ruins.*

But now 'tis near. Before them
the ancient tops of white-stone Moscow
already glow
with golden crosses, ember-bright.
Ah, chums, how pleased I [Onegin] was
when, all at once, the hemicircle
of churches and of belfries,
of gardens, domes, opened before me!
How often during woeful separation,
in my wandering fate,
Moscow, I thought of you!
Moscow! . . . How much within that sound
is blended for a Russian heart!
How much is echoed there!

Here is, surrounded by its park,
Petrovskiy Castle. Somberly
it prides itself on recent glory.
In vain Napoleon, intoxicated
with his last fortune, waited
for kneeling Moscow with the keys
of the old Kremlin: no,
to him my Moscow did not go
with craven brow;
not revelry, not gifts of *bienvenue* —
a conflagration she prepared
for the impatient hero.
From here, in meditation sunk,
he watched the formidable flame.

ALEKSANDR S. PUSHKIN
Eugene Onegin, 1831

"THEY ARE BOMBARDING THE KREMLIN!"

In November 1917, a carefully organized and skillfully executed Bolshevik coup toppled the dissension-ridden Provisional Government that had supplanted the monarchy in March. The remarkable events surrounding that bold bid for power were recorded by an equally remarkable journalist, a Harvard-educated poet named John Reed. In the years immediately preceding the Bolshevik take-over, Reed had ridden with Pancho Villa, fired from a German trench, conducted an open and celebrated affair with the American writer and literary doyenne Mabel Dodge Luhan, and helped found the American Communist Labor Party. In the summer of 1917, the thirty-year-old rake-turned-revolutionary journeyed to Russia, and less than two months after his arrival the Bolshevik uprising began. When it was over, an enthralled and enthusiastic Reed returned to the United States to write his classic account of the coup, Ten Days that Shook the World. *His "slice of intensified history" recorded, Reed returned to Moscow to attend the Second Congress of the Communist International. And it was there, in October of 1920, that he contracted typhus and died. Reed was buried alongside the Kremlin wall, a short distance from the spot where Lenin would be interred.*

They are bombarding the Kremlin!" The news passed from mouth to mouth in the streets of Petrograd, almost with a sense of terror. Travelers from "white and shining little mother Moscow" told fearful tales. Thousands killed; the Tverskaya and the Kuznetsky Most in flames; the church of Vasili Blazheiny a smoking ruin; Usspensky Cathedral crumbling down; the Spasskaya Gate of the Kremlin tottering; the Duma burned to the ground.

Nothing that the Bolsheviki had done could compare with this fearful blasphemy in the heart of Holy Russia. To the ears of the devout sounded the shock of guns crashing in the face of the Holy Orthodox Church, and pounding to dust the sanctuary of the Russian nation. . . .

On November 15th, Lunatcharsky, Commissar of Education, broke into tears at the session of the Council of People's Commissars, and rushed from the room, crying, "I cannot stand it! I cannot bear the monstrous destruction of beauty and tradition. . . ."

That afternoon his letter of resignation was published in the newspapers:

I have just been informed by people arriving from Moscow, what has happened there.

The Cathedral of St. Basil the Blessed, the Cathedral of the Assumption, are being bombarded. The Kremlin, where are now gathered the most important art treasures of Petrograd and of Moscow, is under artillery fire. There are thousands of victims. . . .

What is left? What more can happen? . . .

That same day the White Guards and *yunkers* in the Kremlin surrendered, and were allowed to march out unharmed. . . .

For two days now the Bolsheviki had been in control of the city. The frightened citizens were creeping out of their cellars to seek their dead; the barricades in the streets were being removed. Instead of diminishing, however, the stories of destruction in Moscow continued to grow. . . . And it was under the influence of these fearful reports that we decided to go there. . . .

The station at Moscow was deserted. We went to the office of the Commissar, in order to arrange for our return tickets. He was a sullen youth with the shoulder-straps of a Lieutenant; when we showed him our papers from Smolny, he lost his temper and declared that he was no Bolshevik, that he represented the Committee of Public Safety. . . . It was characteristic — in the general turmoil attending the conquest of the city, the chief railway station had been forgotten by the victors. . . .

Late in the night we went through the empty streets and under the Iberian Gate to the great Red Square in front of the Kremlin. The church of Vasili Blazheiny loomed fantastic, its bright-coloured, convoluted and blazoned cupolas vague in the darkness. There was no sign of any damage. . . . Along one side of the Square the dark towers and walls of the Kremlin stood up. On the high walls flickered redly the light of hidden flames; voices reached us across the immense place, and the sound of picks and shovels. We crossed over.

Mountains of dirt and rock were piled high near the base of the wall. Climbing these we looked down into two massive pits, ten or fifteen feet deep and fifty yards long, where hundreds of soldiers and workers were digging in the light of huge fires.

A young student spoke to us in German. "The Brotherhood Grave," he explained. "To-morrow we shall bury here five hundred proletarians who died for the Revolution."

He took us down into the pit. In frantic haste swung the picks and shovels, and the earth-mountains grew. No one spoke. Overhead the night was thick with stars, and the ancient Imperial Kremlin wall towered up immeasurably.

"Here in this holy place," said the student, "holiest of all Russia, we shall bury our most holy. Here where are the tombs of the Tsars, our Tsar — the People — shall sleep. . . ." His arm was in a sling, from a bullet-wound gained in the fighting. He looked at it. "You foreigners look down on us Russians because so long we tolerated a mediæval monarchy," said he. "But we saw that the Tsar was not the only tyrant in the world; capitalism was worse, and in all the countries of the world capitalism was Emperor. . . ."

As we left, the workers in the pit, exhausted and running with sweat in spite of the cold, began to climb wearily out. Across the Red Square a dark knot of men came hurrying. They swarmed into the pits, picked up the tools and began digging, digging, without a word. . . .

So, all the long night volunteers of the People relieved each other, never halting in their driving speed, and the cold light of the dawn laid bare the great Square, white with snow, and the yawning brown pits of the Brotherhood Grave, quite finished.

We rose before sunrise, and hurried through the dark streets to Skobeliev Square. In all the city not a human being could be seen; but there was a faint sound of stirring, far and near, like a deep wind coming. In the pale half-light a little group of men and women were gathered before the Soviet headquarters, with a sheaf of gold-lettered red banners — the Central Executive Committee of the Moscow Soviets. It grew light. From afar the vague stirring sound deepened and became louder, a steady and tremendous bass. The city was rising. We set out down the Tverskaya, the banners flapping overhead. The little street chapels along our way were locked and dark, as was the Chapel of the Iberian Virgin, which each new Tsar used to visit before he went to the Kremlin to crown himself, and which, day or night, was always open and crowded, and brilliant with the candles of the devout gleaming on the gold and silver and jewels of the ikons. Now, for the first time since Napoleon was in Moscow, they say, the candles were out.

JOHN REED
Ten Days that Shook the World, 1919

PRAISE FOR THE NEW RUSSIA

By his own admission, French novelist André Gide was in love with international communism in general and the U.S.S.R. in particular during the 1930's. In October of 1935 he wrote that it was "the stupidity and the unfairness of the attacks on the U.S.S.R. which made [me] defend it with some obstinacy." And that obstinacy, that blindness to the brutality of Stalin's repressive regime, is very much in evidence in the aging author's description of the crowds gathered in Moscow in 1936 to pay tribute to Russian writer Maxim Gorki.

My domain is the psychological side of things; it is of this especially — of this almost solely — that I mean to treat. If I glance indirectly at social questions, it will still be from a psychological point of view.

. . . The peoples of the Soviet Union are admirable — those of Georgia, of Kakhetia, of Abkhasia, of Ukraine (I mention only those I saw) and even more so to my mind, those of Leningrad and the Crimea.

I was present in Moscow at the Festival of Youth in the Red Square. The ugliness of the buildings opposite the Kremlin was concealed by a mask of streamers and greenery. The whole thing was splendid and — I make haste to say it here, for I shan't always be able to — in perfect taste. The admirable youth of the Soviet Union, gathered together from the North and South, from the East and West, were here on parade. The march past lasted for hours. I had never imagined so magnificent a sight. These perfect forms had evidently been trained, prepared, selected; but how can one fail to admire a country and a regime capable of producing them?

I had seen the Red Square a few days previously on the occasion of Gorki's funeral. I had seen the same people, the same and yet how different! — more like, I imagine, the Russians of the time of the Tzars. They filed past the catafalque in the great Hall of Columns, uninterruptedly, interminably. This time they did not consist of the handsomest, the strongest, the most joyful representatives of the Soviet peoples, but of an indiscriminate concourse of suffering humanity — women, children, children especially, old people sometimes, nearly all of them badly dressed and some looking in the depths of poverty. A silent, dreary, respectful and perfectly orderly procession which seemed to have come up out of the past — a procession which lasted certainly much longer than the other (and glorious) one. I too stayed there a long time watching them. What was Gorki to all these people? I can hardly imagine. A master? A comrade? A brother? At any rate someone who was dead. And on all these faces — even on those of the youngest children — was imprinted a sort of melancholy stupor, but also, and above all, a force, a radiance of sympathy. There was no question here of physical beauty, but how many of the poor people I watched passing by presented me a vision of something more admirable than beauty — how many I should have liked to press to my heart!

Nowhere, indeed, is contact with any and everyone so easily established, so immediately, so deeply, so warmly, as in the U.S.S.R. There are woven in a moment — sometimes a single look suffices — ties of passionate sympathy. Yes, I think that nowhere is the feeling of a common humanity so profoundly, so strongly felt as in the U.S.S.R. In spite of the difference of language, I had never anywhere felt myself so fully a comrade, a brother; and that is worth more to me than the finest scenery in the world.

ANDRÉ GIDE
Back from the U.S.S.R., 1936

In August of 1942, British Prime Minister Winston Churchill paid his lone war-time visit to the Kremlin. The primary purpose of that hastily arranged confer-ence was to assuage Stalin's understandable ire over the Allies' unwillingness — or inability — to open the long-promised second front in Europe. After three days of tense and rather unproductive negotiations, Churchill prepared to depart. As their last formal conversation came to an end, Stalin suddenly and quite un-expectedly insisted that Churchill join him in an impromptu dinner at the Soviet leader's private quarters in the Kremlin. In the fruitful session that followed, the two leaders polished off a steady parade of entrées and a sizable quantity of wine — and drafted a joint Anglo-Soviet communiqué outlining the accord that they had reached in the course of their talks.

Our hour's conversation drew to its close, and I got up to say good-bye. Stalin seemed suddenly embarrassed, and said in a more cordial tone than he had yet used with me, "You are leaving at daybreak. Why should we not go to my house and have some drinks?" I said that I was in principle always in favor of such a policy. So he led the way through many passages and rooms till we came out into a still roadway within the Kremlin, and in a couple of hundred yards gained the apartment where he lived. He showed me his own rooms, which were of moderate size, simple, dignified, and four in number — a dining-room, working-room, bedroom, and a large bathroom. Presently there appeared, first a very aged housekeeper and later a handsome red-haired girl, who kissed her father dutifully. He looked at me with a twinkle in his eye, as if, so I thought, to convey, "You see, even we Bolsheviks have family life." Stalin's daughter started laying the table, and in a short time the housekeeper appeared with a few dishes. Meanwhile Stalin had been uncorking various bottles, which began to make an imposing array. Then he said, "Why should we not have Molotov? He is worrying about the com-muniqué. We could settle it here. There is one thing about Molotov — he can drink." I then realised that there was to be a dinner. I had planned to dine at State Villa No. 7, where General Anders, the Polish commander, was awaiting me, but I told my new and excellent interpreter, Major Birse, to telephone that I should not be back till after midnight. Presently Molotov arrived. We sat down, and, with the two interpreters, were five in number. Major Birse had lived twenty years in Moscow, and got on very well with the Marshal, with whom he for some time kept up a running conversation, in which I could not share.

We actually sat at this table from 8:30 until 2:30 the next morning, which, with my previous interview, made a total of more than seven hours. The dinner was evidently improvised on the spur of the moment, but gradually more and more food arrived. We pecked and picked, as seemed to be the Russian fashion, at a long succession of choice dishes, and sipped a variety of excellent wines. Molotov assumed his most affable manner, and Stalin, to make things go, chaffed him unmercifully.

Presently we talked about the convoys to Russia. This led him to make a rough and rude remark about the almost total destruction of the Arctic convoy in June. I have recounted this incident in its place. I did not know so much about it then as I do now.

"Mr. Stalin asks," said Pavlov [Churchill's second interpreter], with some hesitation, "has the British Navy no sense of glory?" I answered, "You must take it from me that what was done was right. I really do know a lot about the Navy and sea war." "Meaning," said Stalin, "that I know nothing." "Russia is a land animal," I said; "the British are sea animals." He fell silent and recovered his good-humour. I turned the talk on to Molotov. "Was the Marshal aware that his Foreign Secretary on his recent visit to Washington had said he was determined to pay a visit to New York entirely by himself, and that the delay in his return was not due to any defect in the aeroplane, but because he was off on his own?"

Although almost anything can be said in fun at a Russian dinner, Molotov looked rather serious at this. But Stalin's face lit with merriment as he said:

"It was not to New York he went. He went to Chicago, where the other gangsters live."

Relations having thus been entirely restored, the talk ran on. I opened the question of a British landing in Norway with Russian support, and explained how, if we could take the North Cape in the winter and destroy the Germans there, the path of the convoys would henceforth be open. This idea was always, as has been seen, one of my favourite plans. Stalin seemed much attracted by it, and, after talking of ways and means, we agreed we must do it if possible.

WINSTON S. CHURCHILL
The Hinge of Fate, 1950

During the last months of Soviet dictator Joseph Stalin's iron reign, the term "Kremlin watching" had a literal as well as figurative connotation, for during that period of rigorous press censorship and news management, foreign newsmen were often reduced to inferring fluctuations of power within the Kremlin by carefully observing the movement of official limousines through its gates. As Premier Stalin's health began to fail in the early spring of 1953, The New York Times *correspondent Harrison Salisbury sent the first of a series of innocuous-sounding — but highly significant — cables to his editors. Salisbury's prearranged signal alerted New York that the aging leader was gravely ill and that a power struggle among his likely successors was imminent. (Unfortunately for Salisbury, a technical delay in transmitting the key telegram — the one confirming Stalin's death — cost the* Times *its scoop.) Salisbury's* Moscow Journal *augments the censored reports that the veteran reporter filed during Stalin's final illness, and it accurately conveys the profound, nationwide grief that greeted the news of the seventy-four-year-old dictator's death.*

March 4 — 8:30 A.M.

The government announced shortly before eight o'clock this morning that Generalissimo Stalin on Sunday night, March 1-2, suffered a [massive] brain hemorrhage with paralysis of the right hand and leg, loss of speech and of consciousness. . . .

Stalin is said to have been stricken in his quarters in the Kremlin on Sunday night. The illness affected the most important brain centers, disturbing the functions of the heart and lungs. . . .

March 4 — 4:30 P.M. . . .

Those doctors whom I have talked with tell me that a hemorrhage of the extent indicated in the communiqué would have been sufficient to kill outright most men of Stalin's age.

In the interregnum the direction of Soviet affairs has been taken over by that group called Stalin's "closest comrades-at-arms." They have called on the people to display "unity, solidarity, a firm spirit, and vigilance". . . .

No one knows when the next medical bulletin will come out. Radios are turned on constantly. There were long lines at the kiosks — sometimes a hundred and more — to buy papers. Many believers have gone to the churches to pray for Stalin. . . .

March 5 — 1:00 A.M. . . .

Snow-sweeping crews went into action in Red Square where the usual block-long queue of citizens earlier in the afternoon had visited Lenin's Tomb. Spotlights tonight played as always on the red flag flying over the offices of the Supreme Soviet in the Kremlin, and lights burned in the Kremlin offices. The big Council of Ministers' building on Hunter's Row, across from the Moskva Hotel, was a blaze of lights. But this is not unusual. Lights burn in these offices every night of the year.

After I finished filing the initial flashes of the story to New York this morning, I left the telegraph office in the heart of Moscow and walked down to the Red Square. The sun was shining brilliantly on the Moskva River. It was the height of the morning rush hour. Thousands upon thousands of citizens were going to work. There was nothing unusual in the square. Small groups of tourists were being taken around to see the sights. It was hard to realize that just behind the beautiful crenelated Kremlin walls, rosy and golden in the bright March sun, the leader of the Soviet state lay fighting for existence.

Here and there as I went around the city during the day, I saw a woman sobbing as she read the news of Stalin, or a man hastily wiping away a tear. It is hard to describe just what Stalin has meant to the ordinary Russian. But certainly he has never seemed a mere man. . . .

March 5 — 6:30 P.M.

Stalin still lies unconscious while a team of ten medical specialists fight for his life. There is no sign of any turn for the better. Leeches are being used to reduce blood pressure. The press continues to call for all citizens to rally behind the government and maintain "revolutionary vigilance". . . .

March 5 — 10:00 P.M.

The lights are blazing in the windows of the yellow-painted empire buildings of the Kremlin. Heavy traffic flows past, and an icy March wind sweeps across the Moskva River.

I made a circuit of the Kremlin just before 9:00 P.M. The night was bitter, and the wind hurled snow flurries across Red Square and into Menezhnaya Square. The ruby stars . . . glowed red above the Kremlin towers. . . .

March 6 — 7:30 A.M. . . .

The official announcement of Stalin's death was made just after 4:00 A.M. this morning, but only now has the censor begun to pass our dispatches. Death is said to have occurred at 9:50 P.M. last night. . . .

At about 9:30 P.M. — just twenty minutes before Stalin is said to have died — I made a circuit of the Kremlin. There were many cars in Red Square and lots of lights in the buildings. . . .

At 3:30 I drove around the Kremlin again. Saw some government cars in front of the Moscow Soviet building. The woman at *Izvestia* said the paper would be "very late." Just after 4:00 A.M. the chauffeur who was listening to the car radio outside the telegraph office brought in the word of the death. . . .

Pravda has just appeared with broad black borders around the front page, which is devoted entirely to Stalin. There is a large photograph, the official bulletin, the medical reports, and announcement of a funeral commission headed by Khrushchev. . . .

Before the Spassky Gate of the Kremlin in Red Square a crowd of citizens rapidly grew. There were several hundred by 7:30 A.M. On the Hall of Columns a huge portrait was being put up. The red flag which always flies on the Supreme Soviet building behind Lenin's Tomb was lowered to half-staff.

March 6 — 4:30 P.M.

By the time I ventured into Red Square on foot at midmorning the crowds had grown to several thousand. They stood on the sidewalks opposite Lenin's Tomb and in a long half-moon some distance from the Spassky Tower, right in Red Square itself. There were men and women, both young and old, and some children. I had never seen anything like this in Russia before — a *spontaneous* crowd. The throng stood silently, hardly speaking. . . .

Throughout the morning the crowds in the center of the city grew. They were quiet and serious. As early as 7:00 A.M. there was the beginning of a queue at the Hall of Columns in anticipation of Stalin's lying in state. By midmorning that line was several blocks long, and militia were forming the citizens into orderly ranks stretching up Pushkin street. By midafternoon hundreds of thousands of citizens had assembled, and the lines extended back as far as the first garden boulevard. . . .

By 2:00 P.M. the Hall of Columns had been garbed in mourning and powerful floodlights had been installed. MVD regiments had completely cleared out the surrounding squares. . . .

A little before 3:00 P.M. all was in readiness. A single vehicle moved swiftly out of the Kremlin by the Spassky Gate and, circling the center of the city, drew up before the Hall of Columns. Stalin's coffin was borne by a blue vanlike vehicle of the Moscow City Sanitary Department.

Between 3:00 and 4:00 P.M. the leaders of the Communist Party and government entered the Hall of Columns to pay their final respects. At 4:00 the doors were thrown open, and the long, long procession of mourners started past the bier. . . .

March 7 — 4:00 P.M.

Hour after endless hour it goes on — the march of Moscow's mourning millions past Stalin's bier. It started at 4:00 P.M. yesterday and will go on until 2:00 A.M. Monday morning. There has been nothing quite like this before — except when Lenin died in the cold January days of 1924. . . .

The people are fed into the hall eight abreast. Each of the beautiful crystal chandeliers is darkened by gossamer wisps of mourning crepe. In the corridors are countless wreaths. As we ascend the broad staircase, a solid file of guards stands at attention.

The deeper one penetrates, the deeper becomes the ceremonial atmosphere of mourning. Enormous floodlights illuminate the columns. There are cameramen, both movie and still. In the great hall Stalin lies against a bank of thousands of flowers — real, paper, and wax. A symphony orchestra plays funeral music. The line moves swiftly, and it is difficult to see in the dazzling lights who is standing honor guard. Stalin lies, his face placid and quiet, wearing his generalissimo's uniform. . . .

March 7 — 5:30 P.M.

By a series of extraordinary measures the government has transformed the heart of Moscow into a kind of citadel in which almost nothing is going on but mourning for Stalin at the Hall of Columns. . . .

March 8 — 3:30 P.M.

Today is Sunday, and I went over to Red Square just about noon and stood before Lenin's Tomb, watching a band of workmen prepare the mausoleum for Stalin's sarcophagus.

It was an unforgettable experience. The great expanse of the square was empty as I walked up the little hill between the Lenin Museum and the State Historical Museum. Behind me I could hear the distant echo of the crowds thronging to the Hall of Columns.

But inside the great square it was so quiet that each blow of the workmen's hammers rang out like the crash of brass cymbals. Entry to the square was almost blocked by an enormous collection of funeral flowers and wreaths — thousands of them, deposited around the historical museum.

I have often before stood near Lenin's Tomb. But only when the square has been jammed with humanity. Walking across the great space had the quality of a nightmare. But this was no dream. Drawn up before the red and marble mausoleum were three generators. Long cable lines had been run across the square. Inside the tomb workmen were busy. Outside they were replacing the letters on the front which now will spell out Lenin-Stalin instead of just Lenin. . . .

March 9 — 6:00 P.M. . . .

The hour was high noon, and the funeral speeches were over. In the square where the multitude had gathered, there was a moment of utter silence. Then the great golden hands of the clock in Spassky Tower pointed straight up.

The iron bells of Spassky and the steel salute guns of the Kremlin began to speak. Crash! went the bells. Boom! went the cannon. Crash . . . boom . . . crash . . . boom. . . .

Lifting the crimson and black-draped coffin to their shoulders, Stalin's comrades-at-arms bore it inside the mausoleum.

In this last moment they were all there — Malenkov with a deep sadness on his almost youthful face; Beriya, a solid man and solemn; Chou En-lai, flown all the way from China to walk the last steps with Stalin's coffin; Voroshilov, every inch an old comrade; the handsome military figure of Bulganin and the others, Khrushchev, Kaganovich, and Mikoyan.

There were thirty roars of the salute guns — ten per minute — and during those three minutes everything was silent throughout Russia. Every moving vehicle stopped. Every train, every tram, every truck. A single sparrow left its nest high in the Kremlin wall and swooped gracefully over the tomb, its small and gentle chirp sounding strangely loud.

Then roared the voice of General Sinilov, commander of the Moscow garrison, ordering the march-past to begin. There was a shuffle of feet. The crack troops began to move. The military band struck up the triumphant fanfare of Glinka's *Hail to the Czar!* The red flag on the Kremlin was suddenly raised to full staff once more.

Stalin had been laid to rest.

HARRISON SALISBURY
Moscow Journal, 1961

MOSCOW REVISITED

In 1958, Harrison Salisbury returned to Moscow for the first time since Stalin's death. He had left with "a sense of deep relief" following the dictator's demise. Now, after a five-year absence during which he had been denied a visa on the grounds that he had "slandered" the Soviet Union in his news stories, Salisbury was returning to Russia. The Korean conflict had been settled, Khrushchev was in office, and the first Sputniks were in orbit. Russia had changed — to a degree that was to astonish the veteran journalist and longtime Kremlinologist.

Beside the Spassky gate I hesitated, half-tempted to break the ritual of my walk and join the stream of citizens going inside the Kremlin. The first time I had passed through the gate my *propusk* [pass] had been checked by seven security guards. Today I paused at the gate to see if it was really true that anyone could freely pass through the ancient wall and stroll the fairy-tale streets where Russia's history is graven in stone and preserved in mortar and brick. The young army lieutenant and his wife ahead of me paused and asked an attendant with a red arm band. "May one just walk in freely?" the officer asked with deference. "Of course," the guard replied in a tired voice.

So it was true that the Kremlin was a tourist attraction and not a citadel of secret terror. I continued my stroll around the faded pink walls which no longer seemed so grim and frightening. On the grassy banks beside the Tainiye (Secret) Tower I found small boys rolling downhill and girls gathering yellow dandelions and plaiting them into coronets for their hair. Lovers dawdled, and a mother and her child were sunbathing. . . .

I followed the Moskva River embankment to the great Borovitzky gate, oldest of them all, and turned up Kalinin Street. . . .

Often as I walked along the street I halted to snap a picture or jot down a note. It was obvious to all that I was a foreign journalist. But no longer was this a barrier to conversation. Instead, it was an invitation. My walk became a progress from one chat to another. First, talk about American books and authors. Then, surprise that an American would be carrying a Japanese camera. Inquiries from peasants for directions around the city. Approaches by young boys who wanted to practice their English. Another youngster who wanted to talk German. A boy at the book fair who shyly wondered if I had any American books I could spare. No longer was Moscow a silent city. . . .

No doubt Russia was not merely a gay stroller, a troika out to see the Sunday sights, a patron of the new, the bright, and the foreign. Beside the posters of the American shows and the French music, there were advertisements for lectures on Marxism, courses in nuclear physics, and an announcement of the meeting of the local society of atheists. I had seen no police agents and none, I believed, had followed me. But at least one of the young men who stopped to talk to me slipped away quickly with a remark that "It's dangerous." The people looked well dressed in their Sunday clothes and there were foreign foods in the shop windows — Bulgarian peas and tomatoes, Chinese canned fruit, Hungarian sausages. But I would never mistake Kalinin Street for Main Street in any American town. . . .

No, not everything had changed. But much had. Very much. And the changes were in the right direction, changes toward a better life for the Russians, less tension, less strain, less force. They were changes which we as Americans could only welcome.

HARRISON SALISBURY
To Moscow — and Beyond, 1959

*In February 1945 Soviet counter-intelligence agents arrested Aleksandr I. Solzhe-
nitsyn on the charge that he had slandered Stalin in his correspondence with other
Russian men of letters. After a brief incarceration in Moscow, the outspoken
novelist was remanded to Mavrino, a combination prison and research institute
that figures prominently in* The First Circle, *Solzhenitsyn's titanic condemnation
of the Soviet system. In the following excerpt from that novel, which won its
author a Nobel Prize for literature in 1970, a doomed official wanders through
the streets of Stalin's Moscow at dusk.*

The crenelations of the Kremlin walls and the tops of the spruces beside
them were touched with frost. The asphalt was gray and slippery. The mist
seemed to be trying to disappear beneath their wheels.

They were about 200 yards away from the wall, from the wall's teeth, from
the guard behind whom — as they might have imagined — the Greatest Man
on Earth was ending his night. But they passed without even thinking about
him.

When they had driven past St. Basil's Cathedral and turned left onto the
Moscow River embankment, the driver slowed down and asked, "Would
you like to go home, Comrade Colonel?"

That was precisely where he should be going. He probably had left fewer
nights at home than fingers on his hands. But as a dog goes off to die by itself,
Yakonov had to go anywhere but home to his family.

The Pobeda stopped. Gathering up the skirts of his thick leather coat as
he got out, he said to the driver, "You, brother, go home and sleep. I'll get
home by myself."

He sometimes called the driver "brother," but there was such grief in his
voice it was as though he were saying good-bye forever.

A blanket of mist covered the Moscow River to the top of the embankment.

Without buttoning his coat, and with his colonel's high-peaked fur hat
tipped a bit to one side, Yakonov, slipping a little, made his way along the
embankment. . . .

This was where the Yauza River flowed into the Moscow River. Yakonov
crossed the short bridge, still not trying to figure out where he was. . . .

He stood at the parapet of the embankment and looked down. The mist
lay on the ice, not concealing it, and directly below, where it had melted,
Yakonov could see a black hole of moving water. . . .

Abruptly he stepped back from the parapet, out across the embankment
boulevard, and started to climb steeply uphill. A well-trampled path skirted
the fence of still another construction project; it was coated with ice, but
it was not very slippery. . . .

Yakonov made his way up the vacant lot, not noticing where he was going,
not noticing the rise. Finally, shortness of breath brought him to a stop. His
legs were tired, his ankles strained from the unevenness of the ground.

And then, from the high spot he had climbed to, he looked around him
with eyes which now perceived what they saw, and tried to work out where
he was.

In the hour since he had left his car, the night had gotten colder; it was
almost over. The mist had lifted and disappeared. The ground beneath his
feet was strewn with pieces of brick, gravel, broken glass, and there was a
crooked wooden shed or booth near him. Below was the fence along which he

had walked, surrounding a large area where construction had not yet begun. And, though there was no snow, it all loomed white with hoarfrost.

On that hill so near the center of the capital, which had undergone some strange devastation, white steps rose, about seven of them, then stopped, then, it seemed, began again.

Some dull recollection stirred Yakonov at the sight of those white steps on the hill. He climbed them uncomprehending, and continued up the hard-packed cinder pile above them, and then up more steps. They led to a building, dimly outlined in the darkness, a building of strange form, which appeared to be ruined yet, at the same time, whole.

Were these bomb ruins? But there were no such places left in Moscow. Other forces had visited ruin on this place.

A stone landing separated one flight of steps from the next. And now big stone fragments obstructed his climb. The steps led up to the building in rises, like the entrance to a church.

They ended in broad iron doors, shut tight and piled knee-deep with caked gravel.

Yes, yes! The memory lashed Yakonov. He looked around. The river, a curving line of lights, wound far below, its strangely familiar bend disappearing under the bridge and continuing beyond it, toward the Kremlin.

But the bell tower? It was not there. And those piles of stone — were they all that was left of it?

Yakonov's eyes grew hot. He squinted.

He sat down gently on the stone fragments which littered the church portico.

Twenty-two years before he had stood on this very place with a girl called Agniya.

He pronounced her name aloud — Agniya — and, like a breath of air, completely fresh and long-forgotten sensations stirred in his middle-aged, well-fed body.

He had been twenty-six then and she twenty-one. . . .

That same fall they were walking one early evening along the side streets off Taganka Square, when Agniya said in her woodsy voice, which was difficult to hear above the city roar, "Would you like me to show you one of the most beautiful places in Moscow?"

She led him up to a fence surrounding a small brick church which was painted white and red, whose sanctuary, with the main altar, backed on a crooked, nameless side street. Inside the fence there was only a narrow pathway circling the tiny church for processions of the Cross, just wide enough for the priest and the deacon to walk side by side. Through the grated windows of the church one could see, deep inside, the peaceful flames of altar candles and colored icon lamps. And at one corner inside the fence grew a large old oak, taller than the church. Its branches, already yellow, overshadowed even the cupola and the side street, making the church seem very tiny indeed.

"That's the church of St. John the Baptist," said Agniya.

"But it's not the most beautiful place in Moscow."

"Just wait."

She led him through the gate posts into the courtyard. The flagstones were covered with yellow and orange oak leaves. In the shadow of the oak stood an ancient, tent-shaped bell tower. The tower and the little house attached to the church blocked the already sinking sun. The iron double doors of the north vestibule were open, and an old pauper woman standing there bowed and crossed herself at the radiant singing of vespers from within. . . .

"Look!" said Agniya, freeing herself from his arm and drawing him closer to the main portico. They came out of the shadow into a blaze of light from the setting sun, and she sat down on the low stone parapet.

Yakonov drew in his breath. It was as if they had suddenly emerged from the crowded city onto a height with a broad, open view into the distance. A long, white stone stairway fell away from the portico in many flights and landings, down the hill to the Moscow River. The river burned in the sunset. On the left lay the Zamoskvorechye, casting blinding yellow reflections from its windows, and below, almost at one's feet, the black chimneys of the Moscow Electric Power Plant poured smoke into the sunset sky. Into the Moscow River flowed the gleaming Yauza; beyond it to the right stretched the Foundling Hospital; and behind rose the sharp contours of the Kremlin. Still farther off the five gilded cupolas of the Cathedral of Christ the Saviour flamed in the sun.

And in this golden radiance Agniya, with a yellow shawl around her shoulders and seeming golden, too, sat looking into the sun.

"How well the old Russians chose sites for churches and monasteries!" she said, her voice breaking. "I've been down the Volga River, and down the Oka, too, and everywhere they're built on the most majestic sites."

"Yes, that's Moscow!" Yakonov echoed.

"But it's disappearing, Anton," said Agniya. "Moscow is disappearing."

"What do you mean, disappearing? That's nonsense."

"They're going to tear this church down," Agniya persisted.

"How do you know they're going to tear it down?" he said, growing angry. "It's an architectural monument; they'll leave it." He looked at the tiny tentlike bell tower, where the oak branches almost touched the bells.

"They'll tear it down!" Agniya predicted with conviction, sitting as immobile as before, in her yellow shawl in the yellow light. . . .

Yakonov awoke from his reverie. He was sitting on the portico of the Church of St. John the Baptist on a mound of jagged fragments, dirtying his leather coat.

Yes, for no real reason they had wrecked the tent-shaped bell tower and the stairs descending to the river. It was incredible that this December dawn was breaking on the same square yards of Moscow earth where they had been that sunny evening. But the view from the hill was still as distant, and the bends in the river traced by the lamps were just the same.

ALEKSANDR I. SOLZHENITSYN
The First Circle, 1968

REFERENCE

Chronology of Russian History

Entries in boldface refer to the Kremlin.

1147	First mention of Moscow in the Russian Chronicles
1156	**First Kremlin, a wooden stockade, built**
1223	Battle of the Kalka River; Tatars establish their supremacy in Russia
1238	**Batu, Genghis Khan's grandson, burns city of Moscow and the Kremlin**
1240	Alexander "Nevsky" defeats Swedish Army at the Neva River
1242	Nevsky vanquishes the Teutonic knights in the battle of Lake Peipus
1272	**Nevsky's son, Prince Daniel, inherits principality of Moscow and the Kremlin**
1326	**Cornerstone laid of Cathedral of the Assumption**
1326–33	**Cathedral of the Archangel Michael erected**
1328	Metropolitan see officially transferred from Vladimir to Moscow; Ivan Kalita ("Moneybags") becomes grand prince
1330	**Church of the Savior in the Forest completed**
1337	**Moscow and much of the Kremlin devastated by an uncontrollable flash fire**
1339	**Ivan Kalita begins rebuilding Kremlin, replacing its pine palisades with oak walls**
1353	Black Death ravages Russia, claiming Ivan's disciple and successor, Simeon the Proud
1359–74	**Grand Prince Dmitri, Ivan's grandson, replaces wooden stockade with stone walls and new towers**
1365	Second burning of Moscow
1368	Lithuanians attack Moscow, burning all houses outside the Kremlin walls
1370	Citizens of Tver, in league with the Lithuanians, burn Kremlin environs a second time
1380	Dmitri defeats Khan Mamai at Kulikovo pole, destroying myth of Tatar invincibility
1382	**Khan Tokhtamysh sacks Moscow, captures Kremlin through deception**
1389	Kremlin spared in third burning of Moscow
1396–1416	**Building of first Cathedral of the Annunciation**
1408–9	**Kremlin walls, mounted with cannon, withstand Tatar raid**
1425–52	Civil war between Muscovite princes
1448	Russian Church breaks with Rome
1471	**Two Russian architects lay the foundations for new Cathedral of the Assumption**
1472	**Unfinished cathedral collapses during earthquake;** Ivan III (the Great) marries Zoë Palaeologa
1474	Ivan dispatches first mission to Venice to hire architects to construct new Kremlin
1475	**Aristotele Fieraventi arrives in Moscow, begins**

	rebuilding the Cathedral of the Assumption
1478	**Cathedral of the Assumption completed**
1482–90	**Construction of second Cathedral of the Annunciation, designed by Russian architects; Marco Ruffo and Pietro Solario reconstruct Kremlin walls and towers**
1484–93	Additional envoys dispatched to secure assistance of Western European artisans
1487–91	**Palace of Facets and lower section of Savior Tower, Kremlin's main gate, finished**
1490	**Forest Gate built by Solario, chief architect of the Italianate Kremlin**
1493	**Ivan III evacuates fire-damaged quarters in Kremlin**
1505	**Alevisio Novi commissioned to rebuild the Cathedral of the Archangel Michael; death of Ivan the Great**
1508	**First section of Terem Palace finished**
1510	Moat built along east side of Kremlin
1515	**Frescoes of Cathedral of the Assumption finished**
1533	Accession of Ivan IV (the Terrible)
1534–38	Masonry walls erected around the perimeter of the Kitai Gorod, Moscow's trade center
1547	**Ivan IV crowned Tsar and Autocrat of All the Russias in the Cathedral of the Assumption;** fire destroys 25,000 dwellings in Moscow and badly damages the Cathedral of the Annunciation
1549	First *zemski sobor* (parliament) convened
1552	Ivan captures Tatar stronghold of Kazan
1553	**English adventurer Richard Chancellor visits the Kremlin;** Muscovy Company established
1556	Astrakhan, last Tatar enclave, falls to Ivan's army
1560	**Cathedral of Saint Basil the Blessed consecrated;** Moscow dubbed "the Third Rome"
1565	**Foreign Office constructed within Kremlin walls;** Reign of Terror begins
1571	Crimean Tatars plunder Moscow
1581	Ivan accidentally kills his son and heir
1584	Death of Ivan the Terrible; appointment of Boris Godunov as Lord Protector
1586	**Forty-ton *Tsar pushka*, world's largest cannon, cast in Moscow and displayed in Cathedral Square**
1589	Metropolitan of Moscow elevated to the rank of patriarch
1591	Muscovites repel last serious Tatar incursion
1598	Boris Godunov elected tsar
1600–1603	**Belfry of Ivan the Great erected during severe famine in Moscow**

Genealogy: the Romanov Dynasty

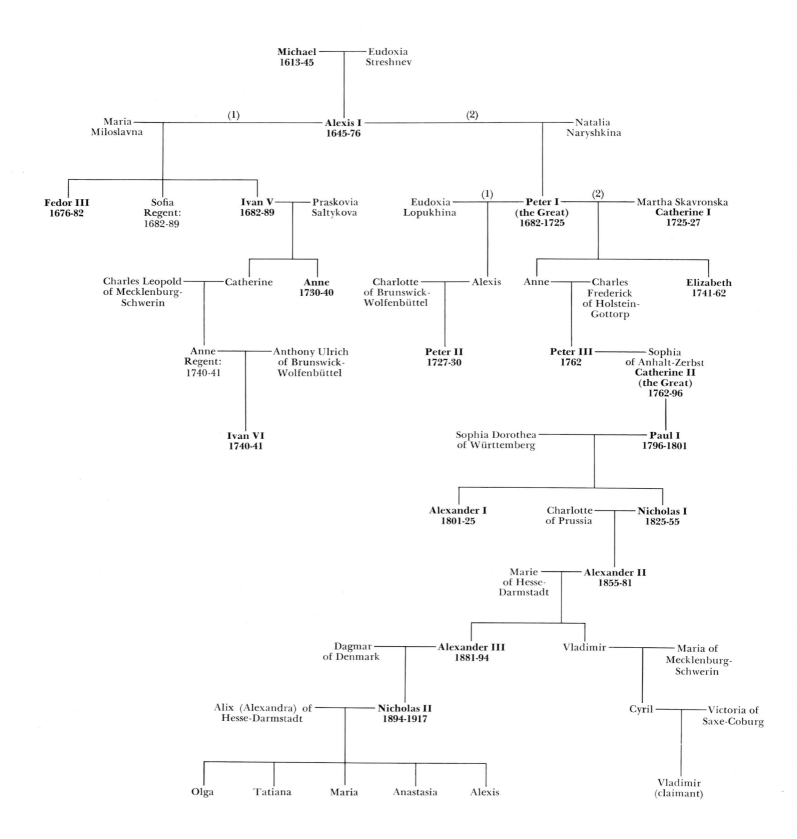

Guide to the Kremlin

Eight centuries of continual construction, renovation, and restoration have transformed Moscow's first wooden citadel into one of the most imposing, intriguing, and awe-inspiring fortresses in the world. Behind the modern Kremlin's formidable walls, buildings as old as the fourteenth-century Church of the Savior in the Forest — last remnant of the original structure — stand alongside such austerely modern buildings as the Palace of Congresses. To reach those buildings, a visitor must pass through one of five steepled gate towers, the tallest and handsomest of which is the *Savior Tower* (1 in the diagram on page 167). That tower, which takes its name from the image of Christ over its chief portal, has been the formal entrance to the inner Kremlin for nearly five centuries. The gate was completed in 1491 by an Italian architect named Pietro Solario, and during the first few decades of the sixteenth century the walls and ceiling of its central arch were covered with elaborate frescoes. About a century later an English clockmaker named Christopher Halloway was commissioned by Tsar Michael Romanov to add a flamboyant Gothic superstructure to Solario's squat gate tower. Halloway's ten-story, 238-foot-high steeple holds an intricate clockwork, chimes, and a network of secret passageways, many of which have never been fully explored.

The Corner Arsenal Tower (2), which stands at the northernmost tip of the Kremlin compound, is perhaps the most imposing of all the fortress's towers. Set on a round rather than a square base, this strategically situated fortress-tower measures a full 168 feet in girth and stands more than 200 feet high. Moreover, the tapering cylinder covers the only functioning underground reservoir left in the Kremlin — out of a score that once supplied water to besieged inhabitants of the citadel.

Trinity Tower (3), across the Kremlin enclosure from the Savior Tower, strongly resembles the latter in shape and pseudo-Gothic detailing, but lacks the Savior Tower's height and graceful lines. A low bridge connects Trinity Tower to *Kutafya Gate* (4), the formal western entrance to the Kremlin. That bridge originally spanned the Neglinnaia River, but between 1817 and 1819 the riverbed was paved over and its flow was diverted underground. Trinity Tower was completed four years after its near-twin across the enclosure — and two centuries later a steeple was added to the blockhouse gate. During that period the cellars beneath the tower served as dungeons.

The Forest Tower (5) is the most distinctive of the Kremlin towers. Its massive base and four stepped tiers are decorated in a distinctly Russian manner, one that may have its origin in the unique designs of medieval Russia's wooden churches. The tower is capped by a 196-foot-high, green-tiled steeple (damaged during the French army's 1812 occupation of Moscow). The Forest Gate, which has the rather dubious distinction of being the portal through which Napoleon entered the Kremlin in 1812, stands nearest the site of the original fortress. Its historical significance notwithstanding, the Forest Gate is an unimposing edifice; it is the only one of the gates not surmounted by a tower.

The adjacent *Water-pumping Tower* (6), as its name implies, once supplied both the Kremlin palaces and gardens with a steady supply of water, which was pumped to its destination through an elaborate system of lead pipes. Built in 1480, the 186-foot-high tower was pulled down and substantially rebuilt in 1805. Seven years later the refurbished structure was destroyed by the French army as it abandoned Moscow. (The *First Nameless* and *Peter* towers (7, 8), also set into the Kremlin's north wall, were damaged by Napoleon's demolition teams at that time.) When the Water-pumping Tower was reconstructed in 1817, Tsar Alexander I appointed Osip Ivanovich Beauvais to give it an Empire façade.

The *Tsar Tower* (9) is the smallest of the Kremlin towers, and its date of construction — 1680 — makes it the youngest as well. The slim, ornate spire is set on the Kremlin wall at the spot where Ivan the Terrible once sat on a raised wooden platform to watch the mass executions in Red Square.

The most famous of the half-dozen white stone churches ringing Cathedral Square is the five-domed *Cathedral of the Assumption* (10). That church, which is modeled on the twelfth-century cathedral at Vladimir, is known as the Reims of Russia. From 1326 to 1700 all of Russia's metropolitans and patriarchs were buried there, and from the sixteenth century, all of Russia's tsars were crowned there. Constructed in 1326 during the reign of Ivan Kalita and extensively rebuilt during the reign of Ivan the Great, the small cathedral subsequently served as a repository for the nation's holiest relics; at one time the church reliquary purportedly contained the robe of Christ, the chains of the Apostle Peter, and the remains of John the Baptist. By 1515 the entire interior of the cathedral had been decorated with frescoes, and when Moscow's boyars entered the resplendent nave for the first time, they reportedly exclaimed, "We see Heaven!" The sumptuous appointments of the Cathedral of the Assumption include a five-tier, fifty-two-foot-high iconostasis covered in chased silver and ornamented with dozens of invaluable icons.

During the 1812 occupation, Napoleon quartered his cavalry troops and their mounts in the cathedral. Before they departed, the French melted down some five tons of silver and gold religious objects and decorations. The nearby *Cathedral of the Annunciation* (11), smallest and most tastefully decorated of all the Kremlin churches, was constructed between 1396 and 1416 and rebuilt on the same site from 1482 to 1490 by architects from Pskov. Its elegant decor includes a floor of inlaid jasper and agate and a series of magnificent frescoes executed in 1405 by Prokhov and Rublev, Russia's preeminent religious painters.

The blaze that swept the Kremlin in 1547 heavily damaged the exterior of this cathedral; in rebuilding, open porches — the first to be attached to any Russian church — were added on three sides. At the same time two additional domes were affixed to the cathedral roof (bringing the total to nine) and the entire cluster was first sheathed in copper and then gilded.

The richly adorned *Cathedral of the Archangel Michael* (12), directly across Cathedral Square from the Cathedral of the Annunciation, is the third church dedicated to the archangel to stand on that site. The first wooden structure, built in 1250, was demolished less than a century later and rebuilt in stone. In 1505 Ivan the Great commissioned an Italian architect to erect a third cathedral on the spot. The building was finished four years later, and since that time it has served as both royal chapel and royal crypt. Forty-seven tsars — from Ivan the Great to Peter the Great — are buried in its vaults. (One notable exception is the seventeenth-century tsar Boris Godunov, whose mortal remains are interred elsewhere.)

Following his marriage to Zoë Palaeologa in 1472, Ivan the Great set in motion a grand scheme to convert Moscow into "the Third Rome." Among other tasks assigned Ivan's phalanx of Italian craftsmen was that of erecting a suitable dwelling for the tsar. That palace, known as the *Palace of Facets* (13), was completed in 1491 by Solario. The royal residence — the oldest civil structure in Moscow — takes its name from the harlequinade brickwork patterns on its façade. Its most striking feature is an enormous reception room — nearly seventy feet square and dominated by a massive, gilded central pillar — that occupies the entire second story of the palace. In that vast, vaulted throne room Ivan IV feted his victory over Kazan in 1552 and Peter the Great toasted his triumph over the Swedes at Poltava in 1709.

In 1508, three years after Ivan the Great's death, the first section of the *Terem Palace* (14) was completed. Its carved and painted portals and parapets, stained-glass windows, and huge tiled stoves represent a remarkable synthesis of the decorative arts of fifteenth-century

Russia. In the decade between 1839 and 1849, the Terem Palace was incorporated into Konstantin Ton's ambitious design for the *Grand Kremlin Palace* (15). Ton's grandiose plan linked the Terem Palace and the Palace of Facets into a single imperial residence covering half a million square feet. The Grand Kremlin Palace, largest building in the complex, includes three formal reception halls dedicated to saints Vladimir, George, and Alexander.

During Catherine the Great's long reign, the triangular *Senate Building* (16) was added to the northwest corner of the Kremlin compound. That building, which today houses the Council of Ministers, was considered an excellent example of Russian classical architecture when it was erected between 1776 and 1787. Due west of the Senate Building lies the *Arsenal Building* (17), a severely classical structure erected by Peter the Great on the site of the Kremlin granaries, which burned down in 1701. It was Peter's intention that the Arsenal Building serve as a war museum, and after the 1709 battle of Poltava he sent samples of captured Swedish arms there. The tsar's project died with him, however, and it was the *Armory Building* (18), also designed by Ton, that eventually became the official Kremlin museum. Originally an arsenal and later a workshop for artisans, the Armory was gradually converted into a storehouse for imperial collections. Royal armor, state carriages, furniture, clothing, jewelry, and plate are displayed there today.

South of the Arsenal stands the *Kremlin Palace of Congresses* (19), a large, modern, post-Revolutionary structure. This austere glass and marble administrative building, which contains some eight hundred small offices and a main hall seating six thousand, was officially opened on October 17, 1961, the forty-fourth anniversary of the Bolshevik coup d'etat.

Over the centuries, personal whim and national pride led to the construction of a number of other Kremlin monuments. Among them is the *Belfry of Ivan the Great* (20), which was completed by Boris Godunov's engineers during the famine of 1600–1603 as a testament to the piety of its builder. The 270-foot-high tower, tallest in the Kremlin, is hung with thirty-three bells, all decorated with copious relief work.

The *Tsar Cannon* (21), cast in Moscow in 1586, is sixteen feet long and weighs more than forty-two tons. This huge artillery piece was commissioned by Tsar Fedor and bears his portrait in bas-relief on its highly decorated sides. Although intended only for decorative purposes,

the cannon was provided with a supply of cannonballs, each a yard in diameter.

Large as it is, the Tsar Cannon cannot compare in size with the enormous *Tsar Bell* (22). Cast during the first decade of the seventeenth century for Boris Godunov, the massive bell supposedly hung in the Tsar Tower during the reign of Aleksei Mikhailovich. According to Russian legend, it fell during the fire of 1737, sundered, and then lay half-buried until 1836, when it was excavated and mounted on its present granite base.

The vast plaza that flanks the Kremlin's western wall has played an integral role in the citadel's history. It is no surprise, therefore, that Alexander I began the task of rebuilding his gutted capital after Napoleon's retreat by refurbishing the great square. For centuries *Red Square* (23) had served as an open market, political forum, parade ground, and open-air dock. Numerous political prisoners were executed at the *Place of Skulls* (24), a raised platform that also served as an altar for certain religious rites. In 1547 Ivan the Terrible knelt alone on this low brick rostrum and repented his multitudinous sins, and in 1698, during the last *streltsy* revolt, Peter the Great used the same spot for the execution of countless rebels.

At the opposite end of Red Square stands what is unquestionably Moscow's most striking building, the *Cathedral of Saint Basil the Blessed* (25). Erected between 1553 and 1560 to celebrate Ivan the Terrible's victory over the Tatar stronghold of Kazan, this remarkable, multihued church stands over the grave of Moscow's holy beggar, Saint Basil. Around the central church stand nine auxiliary churches — eight built by Ivan to commemorate his eight decisive victories over the Tatars, and a ninth added in 1588 to house the remains of Saint Basil. Collectively, the ten churches duplicate on an exaggerated scale — and in masonry — the exuberant ornamentation of Russia's celebrated wooden churches.

In the seventeenth century Saint Basil the Blessed's distinctive onion domes were painted in rainbow colors, leading enthusiastic onlookers to compare the cathedral to a rare tropical plant — and prompting one critic to liken the church to an "overinflated frog at the instant of explosion."

The Lenin Mausoleum (26), a squat and unadorned reviewing stand and crypt of highly polished red marble, was begun in 1925, the year after Lenin's death. Since that time it has become one of the Kremlin's most popular shrines, toured each year by millions of respectful — or simply curious — Russian peasants and foreign visitors.

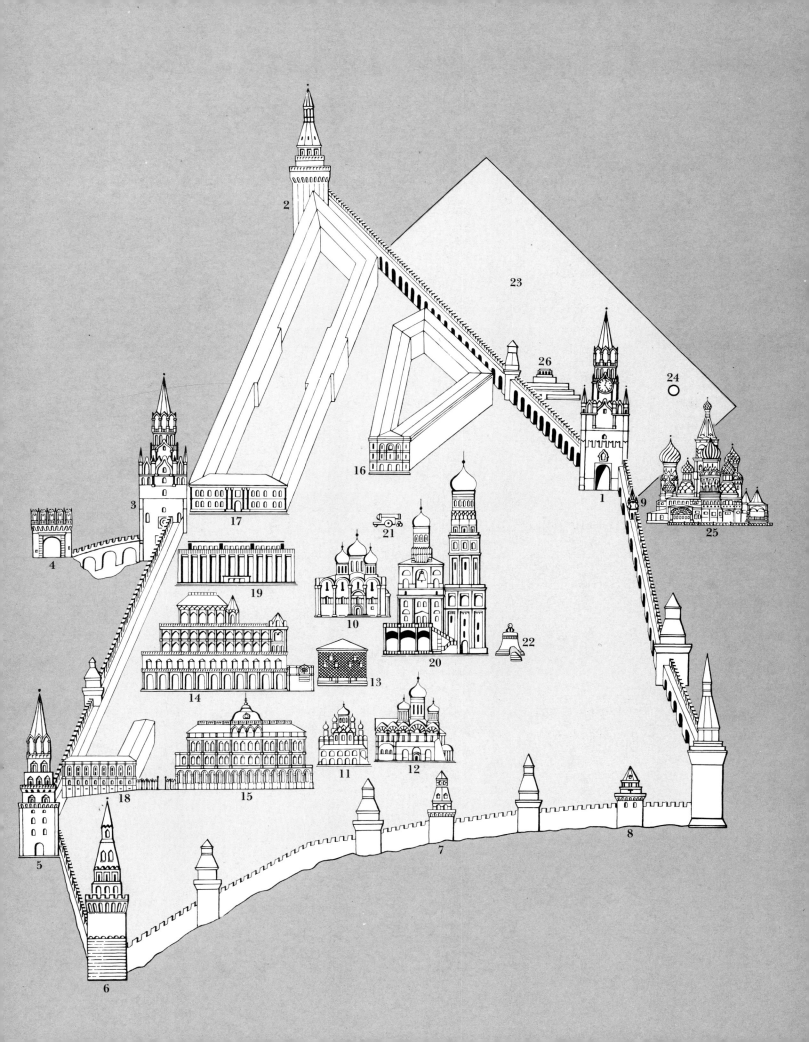

Selected Bibliography

Alexandrov, Victor. *The Kremlin: Nerve-Centre of Russian History*. Translated by Roy Monkcom. New York: St. Martin's Press, 1963.

Catherine the Great. *Memoirs of Catherine the Great*. Translated by Katherine Anthony. New York and London: Alfred A. Knopf, Inc., 1927.

Clarkson, Jesse D. *A History of Russia*. New York: Random House, 1961.

De Caulaincourt, Armand. *With Napoleon in Russia*. New York: William Morrow and Co., 1935.

Fennell, J. L. I. *Ivan the Great of Moscow*. London and New York: Macmillan & Company Ltd. and St. Martin's Press, 1961.

Florinsky, Michael T. *Russia: A History and an Interpretation*. 2 vols. New York: The Macmillan Co., 1955.

Fülöp-Miller, René. *Rasputin: The Holy Devil*. Translated by F. S. Flint and D. F. Tait. Garden City, New York: Garden City Publishing Company, Inc., 1928.

Grey, Ian. *Ivan the Terrible*. Philadelphia and New York: Lippincott, 1964.

Hamilton, George Heard. *The Art and Architecture of Russia*. Baltimore: Penguin Books, 1954.

Korb, Johann Georg. *Scenes from the Court of Peter the Great*. Edited by F. L. Glaser. New York: N. L. Brown, 1921.

Pares, Bernard. *The Fall of the Russian Monarchy*. New York: Alfred A. Knopf, Inc., 1939.

Reed, John. *Ten Days That Shook the World*. New York: Random House, 1960.

Riasanovsky, Nicholas V. *A History of Russia*. New York: Oxford University Press, 1963.

Sumner, Benedict Humphrey. *Peter the Great and the Emergence of Russia*. New York: Collier Books, 1966.

Tarlé, Eugene. *Napoleon's Invasion of Russia, 1812*. "Translated by G. M." London: George Allen & Unwin, Ltd., 1942.

Vernadsky, George. *The Mongols and Russia*. New Haven: Yale University Press, 1953.

————. *The Tsardom of Moscow, 1547–1682*. 2 vols. New Haven and London: Yale University Press, 1969.

Voyce, Arthur. *The Moscow Kremlin: Its History, Architecture, and Art Treasures*. Berkeley: University of California Press, 1954.

Waliszewski, K. *The Romance of an Empress. Catherine II of Russia*. New York and London: D. Appleton and Company, 1929.

Acknowledgments and Picture Credits

The Editors make grateful acknowledgment for the use of excerpted material from the following works:

Back from the U.S.S.R. by André Gide. Translated by Dorothy Bussy. Copyright 1937 by Martin Secker & Warburg Ltd. The excerpt appearing on page 151 is reproduced by permission of Martin Secker & Warburg Ltd. and Alfred A. Knopf, Inc.

"Eugene Onegin" by Aleksandr S. Pushkin. Translated by Vladimir Nabokov. Copyright 1964 by the Bollingen Foundation. The excerpt appearing on page 148 is reproduced by permission of Princeton University Press.

Memoirs of Catherine the Great. Translated and edited by Katherine Anthony. Copyright 1927 by Alfred A. Knopf, Inc. and renewed 1955 by Katherine Anthony. The excerpt appearing on pages 141-42 is reproduced by permission of Alfred A. Knopf, Inc.

Moscow Journal by Harrison E. Salisbury. Copyright 1961 by Harrison E. Salisbury. The excerpt appearing on pages 153-56 is reproduced by permission of the University of Chicago Press.

The First Circle by Aleksandr I. Solzhenitsyn. Translated from the Russian by Thomas P. Whitney. Copyright 1968 by Harper & Row, Publishers, Inc. English translation copyright 1968 by Harper & Row, Publishers, Inc. The excerpt appearing on pages 158-60 is reproduced by permission of Harper & Row, Publishers.

The Hinge of Fate by Winston S. Churchill. Copyright 1950 by Houghton Mifflin Company. The excerpt appearing on pages 152-53 is reproduced by permission of Houghton Mifflin Company and Cassell and Company Ltd., which published the book as *The Second World War*.

To Moscow—and Beyond by Harrison E. Salisbury. Copyright 1959, 1960 by Harrison E. Salisbury. The excerpt appearing on page 157 is reproduced by permission of Harper & Row, Publishers.

War and Peace by Leo Tolstoi. Translated by Louise and Aylmer Maude. Copyright 1942 by Simon and Schuster. The excerpt appearing on pages 145-48 is reproduced by permission of Oxford University Press.

The Editors would like to thank the following organizations and individuals for their assistance:

A la Vieille Russie, New York — Peter Shaffer
Jay Axelbank, Moscow

Marilyn Flaig, New York
Kate Lewin, Paris
Novosti, Moscow — A. Porozhniakov
Erroll Rainess, New York
Ellen Rooney, New York
Elena Whiteside, New York

The title or description of each picture appears after the page number (boldface), followed by its location. Photographic credits appear in parentheses. The following abbreviations are used:

ALT,NYPL — Astor, Lenox and Tilden Foundations, New York Public Library
BM   — British Museum
NYPL   — New York Public Library
(N)   — (Novosti)
(ER)   — (Erroll Rainess)
RBD,NYPL — Rare Books Division, New York Public Library
R,SRI   — A.D. Rovinski, *Sources of Russian Iconography,* 1884-98, New York Public Library
SHM,M   — State Historical Museum, Moscow
STG,M   — State Tretyakov Gallery, Moscow

ENDPAPERS Set design for the 1910 Paris production of Igor Stravinsky's ballet *Firebird* by A. Golovin. STG,M HALF TITLE Symbol designed by Jay J. Smith Studio FRONTISPIECE Icon of "The Spreading of the Tree of the State of Moscow" by Simon Ushakov, 1668. STG,M (N)   9 Menu of the coronation dinner of Nicholas II, from *Les Solennités du Saint Couronnement . . . ,* St. Petersburg, 1899. RBD,NYPL   10-11 Photograph of the Kremlin floodlit for the 51st anniversary of the Russian Revolution (N)   12-13 Icon of "The Church Militant," mid-16th century. STG,M (Editions Circle d'Art)

CHAPTER I   16 Icon of the battle between Novgorod and Suzdal in 1169, *c.* 1460. Museum of History, Novgorod (Nouvelle Librairie de France)   18 Painting of Alexander Nevsky on a pillar in the Cathedral of the Archangel Michael, 17th century (N)   19 Icon of the Vladimir Madonna, 12th century. STG,M   20 Miniature of the building of a bridge over the Moscow River, from the *Tsar's Book.* SHM,M (N)   21 Three miniatures showing the building of the Kremlin, from a manuscript by Nikonov Letopis. SHM,M (N)   22, 23 Two miniatures showing Ivan Kalita holding court and punishing a boyar, from *The Life of Sergei Radonezhsky,* 16th century. Lenin Library, Moscow (N)   24, 25 Two reconstructions of the Kremlin, by A. Vasnetsov: left, in the time of Ivan Kalita; right, in the time of Dmitri Donskoi. Museum of History and Reconstruction, Moscow (N)   26 Miniature showing Dmitri Donskoi reviewing his troops, from *The Tale of the Bloody Encounter with Mamai,* 14th century. BM, Yates Thompson, 51 fol 29v   27 Miniature showing Dmitri Donskoi and his brother, Vladimir, praying, from *The Tale of the Bloody Encounter with Mamai,* 14th century. BM, Yates Thompson 51 fol 14v

CHAPTER II   30 Map of Moscow, from *Civitates Orbis Terrarum* by G. Braun, Cologne, 1591. ALT,NYPL   31 Woodcut of Ivan III, from *Cosmographie Universelle* by A. Thévet, 1555. NYPL   33 Photograph of the Cathedral of the Annunciation at left and the Cathedral of the Assumption at right (ER)   36 Interior of the Palace of Facets (N)   38, 39 Three woodcuts: left, of Russian Tatars; center, of the Russian countryside; right, of Vasili III; from *Commentari della Moscovia* by Sigismund von Herberstein, 1557. ALT,NYPL   40 Icon of saints Vladimir, Boris, and Gleb, 16th century. STG,M   41 Interior of the Cathedral of the Archangel Michael (N)

CHAPTER III   44 The "Kazan Hat" of Ivan IV, 16th century. State Museum of the Kremlin, Moscow   45 Icon of the sack of Novgorod by Ivan IV, 16th century. State Historical Museum, Novgorod (Deutsche Fotothek, Dresden)   46 Miniature showing the departure from the Kremlin of the Tsarina Anastasia, from a manuscript by Nikonov Letopis. SHM,M (N)   47 Miniature showing the building of the new court of Ivan IV, from a manuscript by Nikonov Letopis. SHM,M (N)   48 Icon of Ivan IV, 16th century. National Museum, Copenhagen   50-51 Three photographs of the Cathedral of St. Basil the Blessed (ER)   52 Double-headed eagle from the ivory throne of Ivan IV. The Armory, Moscow (N)   53 Woodcut of Ivan IV and his prisoners, 1582. R,SRI   54-55 Colored engraving of Russian ambassadors from the court of Ivan IV, 1576. R,SRI   57 Detail from the door of the Belfry of Ivan the Great (ER)

CHAPTER IV   61 The Belfry of Ivan the Great (ER)   62 Miniature of Boris Godunov, from the *Titulyarnik,* 1672. SHM,M (N)   64 Painting of the murder of Tsarevich Dmitri, May 15, 1591. Bibliothèque Slav, Paris   65 left, Engraving of the first False Dmitri; right, Engraving of the second False Dmitri (Mary Evans Picture Library)   67 top, The Savior Tower; bottom, The

INDEX